Fall In

A Veteran with a Gambling Addiction

Dave Yeager

Fulton Books
Meadville, PA

Published by Fulton Books 2023

ISBN 979-8-88982-010-9 (paperback)
ISBN 979-8-88982-011-6 (digital)

Printed in the United States of America

Introduction

This is a story of hope. It may not feel like a story of hope at first, but it is. My name is Dave, and I am an eleven-year veteran of the United States Army. I am also in recovery from a gambling addiction. This addiction cost me my career in the Army. It also destroyed my first marriage and nearly destroyed my current marriage. This addiction caused me to lose contact with my children for two years, have multiple suicide attempts, and steal from an employer to the tune of a felony. This is the story of my journey before, during, and in recovery from gambling addiction.

Okay, is gambling really an addiction? Doesn't a compulsive gambler just have some character issues to iron out? Aren't some gamblers just degenerates who can't find any other way to get their thrills? Don't people just gamble to get more money? While some of these things may be true for some people, more often than not, the compulsion to gamble beyond what the average person would gamble is driven by addiction. Gambling addiction, or gambling disorder, is an addiction every bit as real as drugs or alcohol and every bit as devastating if unchecked and untreated for too long. If you ask a lot of people what gambling is, they'll tell you slot machines, poker, roulette, and sports betting. But gambling can also include things like bingo, the stock market, a simple block pool at work, and cryptocurrency. Gambling is risking something of value for something that's perceived to have more value with no guarantee of the outcome. Simply put, gambling is a risk. This risk can be fun for most people. But for some, it can develop into an insatiable drive. Risking something of value doesn't always mean money. Risking anything of value such as time, property, belongings, or even reputation can be considered gambling.

Gambling addiction, much like drugs, alcohol, or any other addiction, feeds on dopamine and ego. Dopamine is a stuff that's already in our bodies that makes us feel good. When something good happens, dopamine is often released and produces a happy feeling. Some of us struggle with uncomfortable feelings. We don't like them, don't want to deal with them, or even flat-out avoid them. A rise in dopamine can temporarily wash those uncomfortable feelings away. So the good feeling of alcohol or certain drugs or a big win at the poker table can create that rise in dopamine and the bad feelings wash away. For the person prone to addiction, this can create a desire to want that feeling again…and again. That's what happened to me, which you'll see later. Ego can be another huge driver of addiction. We want to feel special or different or bigger than life. Addiction can temporarily create that feeling. Standing at the roulette table, on a roll, and surrounded by "adoring fans" can create a moment of bliss. Again, that feels good and the person prone to addiction will likely chase that good feeling, trying to recreate it. Gambling does this as effectively as drugs or alcohol, just without the chemical boost. It's as real as it gets.

Being in the military adds elements that can make us even more prone to addiction. It's a high-paced, often high-stress environment. Military service members entering boot camp or basic training are pretty much taught, from day one, to tuck away fear and other feelings and focus on the accomplishment of the mission. You really can't blame the military. It's kind of an essential element of ensuring the mission gets accomplished, but unfortunately, the service member learns that dealing with feelings is not only unnecessary but can be dangerous. The problem with that is that, eventually, the feelings need to be dealt with, but the service member doesn't have the tools to do that, so they often reach for alternatives such as drinking or gambling. Military service often comes with downtime. In fact, there is more downtime than a lot of people realize. Gambling provides something to fill that downtime, whether it's a poker game in a hooch or dice in the barracks or, in today's high-paced world of gambling, the multitude of ways to gamble that are now available right on our phones, or the three thousand slot machines that are available on military bases overseas. So between the need to escape difficult feelings, the need to fill downtime, the fact that the average age of service members tends to be younger, the warrior ethos that tells us to never give in and never quit, and the opportunities available to service members, it's no surprise that gambling addiction among service members is higher than the general population.

I fell into my addiction to gambling while on active duty in the Army. Many of the things I mentioned above played a role in the development of that addiction. And the addiction was very destructive for me and for my family. Many things before my time in the Army contributed to the development of my addiction. I had anything but a perfect life. While I wish much of it could be different, I can't change any of it. I struggled with a gambling addiction for many years, had a bunch of quiet and even happy years, then struggled again. In the end, what I have discovered is hope and a way to take my addiction and learn from it, learn a better and healthier way to live. That's it. That's what I want to share. I want to tell you how I got into my addiction and what it felt like for me. I do this to make the message clear to anyone who might be struggling that you are not alone. More importantly, I want to share what's working, what has led me to what I consider the healthiest and happiest time in my life, and why I believe I can continue to live in recovery for the rest of my life. Grab a rope and let's do this. This is a story of hope!

Before Gambling

In the Beginning

If this is a story about my journey through gambling addiction, why talk about what happened before I started gambling? Well, it's important to understand that many of the beliefs and habits and unhealthy things that I did during my gambling addiction were put in place long before I started gambling. There are those who would say knowing why an addicted gambler started gambling isn't important, just that it did, and it needs to come to an end. While I can understand the sentiment, I don't agree. For me, understanding what was behind my desire to gamble goes a long way toward helping unravel what's beneath the addiction and ultimately strengthen my recovery.

There is so much more to my story of growing up I could write a book about just that, and someday I just might. But for the purposes of this book, I'm going to give you enough to gain a better understanding of my past. I did not spend a lot of time in one place. I was born in Philadelphia, Pennsylvania. I have vague memories of living there, but my mother divorced my father when my brothers and I were very young. I may have been four or so when we moved from Philly to coastal New Jersey. We lived with my grandmother for a while until my mother could find a place to rent. We moved in and it wasn't long after that Mom started dating. My aunt introduced my mother to a friend of the guy she was dating. Both of them were carpenters working in development in the area. He seemed pretty neat at first, at least from what I could remember. He would spend time with my mother and goof around with my brothers and me. I do remember a lot of drinking, but it was the seventies and that was hardly unusual. I don't how long they dated before they got married, but I don't remember it being very long. They got married at our

3

house, and suddenly my brothers and I had a new dad. But it wasn't long until we began to realize this dad was not going to be the father of the year.

A Terrorist State

After my mother and new stepfather got married, he decided he had enough of carpentry in New Jersey and wanted to become a farmer in Pennsylvania. I believe I was about six years old when we packed everything up and moved into a small rental farm about an hour or so outside of Philadelphia. It didn't take long until my brothers and I were put to work. We had to pick up sticks and rocks and feed the animals and shovel manure. At first, it felt almost fun. But not long into it, the fun vanished. If we did not do our assigned work to exact standards, we were punished. The punishment at that time was a belt across the backside. I remember getting that belt often. It didn't feel good. We were also given more and more to do. It didn't matter if it was cold or rainy or nighttime. The work would get done no matter what. Mind you, my brothers and I were all under the age of ten.

We lived on that farm for about a year or two then moved to a bigger one about a half hour or so away, and not long after that, my sister was born. We had to change school districts, but I don't remember making friends in the one we moved from, so it wasn't a big deal. The farm we moved from had less than fifty acres, but we only used the barn and areas right around the house. The new farm was 105 acres, and we would use every bit of it. The house was old and beat up. The bathroom didn't have a shower or a door. It just had an old bathtub, and we put up a shower curtain for the door. The barn seemed like it could fall down at any minute, but it held up. My stepfather wanted to raise crops and hogs. We did both. We quickly had over one hundred pigs on the property, and he began prepping the land for corn and wheat and other crops. I should say *we* began prepping the land. He had very old farm equipment. After he would plow the land, my brothers and I had to walk through the freshly plowed field and pick up rocks. This could be five acres or fifty acres of land. We had to make sure it was rock-free. If it wasn't, we would get punished. Since we were getting older, the belt was no longer the punishment of choice. It was now an open hand to the side of the head. I remember seeing stars almost every time I'd receive one of those. In addition to picking rocks, we would have to feed and clean the hogs, pull weeds in the five-acre vegetable garden, pick up corn that got missed by the very old and very abused corn picker, stand on the hay wagon and stack hay as it got kicked into the wagon from the bailer, and cut and stack wood because we heated our house entirely on wood.

By the time I was about twelve years old, I was a full-time indentured servant on the farm. I say indentured servant because if I wanted to participate in after-school activities like baseball or theater or dances, I had to first finish my assigned work. More often than not, my work was not to "standard," and I would be denied these activities. One thing my brothers and I were allowed to do was play little league baseball. The diamond we played on was two and a half miles away, and we were never offered a ride. We didn't care. The walk gave us extra time to just be us. I was not a very good baseball player. I really didn't care. I just wanted time to try to be a kid. Those times were few and far between, but we took full advantage of them when we got them. We also took full advantage of visitors. Any time family would come to visit, he would act more like a parent, and things would calm down. Finally, we would catch breaks when he went on a drinking binge. These were becoming more frequent and getting longer when they happened. He would go off somewhere and drink himself into a stupor. I still took care of the animals but also made more time for fun.

We had nothing. We were dirt poor, literally. I remember a Christmas when I dug into an old can of pretzels and dug out the salt and remaining crumbs. That's what I ate that day. I also remember getting an old rusted dump truck as a gift. I have to say, I had more fun with that truck than with many of the gifts I had gotten. For my stepfather, the drinking was getting worse. In junior high school, I was allowed to try out for the musical. We had a combined seventh through twelfth grade, so we could all try out. It was seventh grade, and I got a part. It was a small part, but it was a part. I was allowed to go to the necessary nightly rehearsals, but I had to get my own ride. The high school was about forty minutes down the road. I got a ride from my friends who lived up the road and were in the show as well. Each day I would stay after school, and each night they would bring me home. I never invited them in or even close because I didn't want them to see where I lived, how I lived, or whom I lived with. One night, after being dropped off, I was grateful for my approach. I got out of the VW microbus I was in and walked to the back door—we really didn't have a front door—opened it, and found my stepfather there with the stove door open, taking a leak right on it like it was a urinal. I was more embarrassed than I could ever be. I was the kid whose parent pissed on the appliances. No one could ever know.

As I said, the alcoholic binges got worse. What also got worse was the rage he would experience when he decided to dry up from the binge. He detoxed by sleeping for a few days then diving into work. Honestly, it was a nightmare. I remember always having to look down when I spoke to him because if I looked him in the eye, he would take it as a threat, and I would get the crap beat out of me. He would tell us to speak up when we murmured then yell at us for being too mouthy when we did speak up. It always felt like a trap. My younger brother didn't really care. He was a challenger from the day he was born and decided he had no fear. He paid for that lack of fear and took the worst of the beatings. My older brother was the workhorse and the parent of the four of us. He was just plain angry most of the time. We would also be belittled on a daily basis and told we wouldn't amount to anything, so why bother trying? In those years, I learned how to hide. I hid my feelings. I hid my opinions. I hid myself. I masked it all with humor, and the stage was my outlet.

The work and abuse went on for a few more years. When I was fifteen, my stepfather decided, or was forced to decide, that he had enough of farming and was moving an hour south to live in a house his uncle owned and get back into carpentry. I had made friends at my school and didn't want to leave. My older brother felt the same way and arranged to move in with some friends of his. Their mother was a teacher, so it made the decision pretty easy. I figured since my brother had done it, I would do the same thing. I reached out to a friend and trusted community leader in the area. He agreed to take me in. So in my sophomore year of high school, I was finally set free of the tyranny I was living under on the farm, or so I thought.

Out of the Frying Pan

I felt like I was finally free of the stresses of living with an alcoholic and abusive stepfather. I knew I would miss my mother and my siblings. I also knew I desired the freedom to live like a normal teenager, and the gentleman who offered his home and family to me seemed to give me exactly that. At first, it was a pretty cool experience. There was work to do around the house, but I didn't mind it. I was used to work. But it wasn't long until the lady of the house started to become less than friendly to me. She would be abrupt, even yelling at me at times to get my work done. I felt shades of what I had just left. I was able to bear it because otherwise my life was going pretty well. I was in the band and choral groups and doing shows at school. I had friends and was able to do teenaged boy stuff. It all seemed like it would be okay. Then something happened that would haunt me for many years, and still does sometimes. One night I was in my room lying in bed. I was just getting ready to fall asleep when my friend and mentor, the man who offered me a place to live, walked in. The house was quiet, and he put his finger up to his mouth to ensure I would keep it quiet. He then pushed me on my back, pulled down my pajama pants, and performed a sexual act on me. I was shocked and scared, but I let him finish what he was doing because I didn't know what else to do. If I lashed out, I would be on the street at fifteen. But I did not enjoy what was happening at all. My freedom was over. I had a woman who preferred yelling over conversation and a man who played out his sexual fantasies on a boy who, up until that point, looked up to him as a father figure. Not long after that night, I talked to my best friend from school, and I was on the move again.

In the middle of the night, months after I was taken in by a family that I thought would show me what a real family was, I snuck out with everything I could carry, jumped in my friend's car, and we were off to his house. The family I had been staying with never pursued me, and my own family didn't question the move, if they even knew about it. I was quite grateful for that. I didn't want to tell anyone about what happened to me. I was ashamed and embarrassed that I could let something like that happen. I still don't like talking about it, but it's essential to understand that these events and the beliefs created from these events were major contributors to my gambling addiction. I also need to talk about it because it helps me to continue to process and let go of old feelings that I still have about it.

A Few Good Years

The next few years were pretty good years. I was pretty much a normal teenager in high school. I was in the band. I had decent grades. I had a great best friend and a good nighttime job at the local pizza place. I worked summers at a Boy Scout camp. The summer before my senior year, one of my fellow counselors got a visit from his sister on a Friday night. His sister was not alone. She brought a friend with her. She and I immediately connected. I think we could both feel it. Before that summer was over, we were dating. It got quite serious through the first half of our senior year. There was even talk of marriage down the road. At that point, I began to get scared. If we got too serious, I would have to tell her all about myself and my life and my family. I was not going to do that. I had gotten very good at hiding it. So in January of 1985, our senior year, I sat on the front porch of my best friend's house and let her go. I was as kind as I could be, and she would tell me years later that she felt like I was kind. Looking back, I really didn't want to let her go, but the idea of letting her get to really know me scared me way more than the pull of love I felt from her. That love was clearly real because many years later I married that woman. More about that later.

I finished high school and tried a year of college. I again dated someone my freshman year, but once again when things got too intimate, I left. I could be in a crowd all day long. I could entertain hundreds of people and loved it. But put me in a room, one-on-one, and I was as afraid as I could possibly be. People were simply not allowed to know who I was. After a year of college, I didn't go back. I was bored and wanted something more exciting in my life. I went out and worked a few odds and ends jobs. I wasn't satisfied with anything. One day, I was driving from the mall and saw an Army recruiting office in a strip mall. I decided to go in and check it out. After an hour with the recruiter, I discovered the Army was way more than guns and grenades and that I could get a job as a musician. So, I started the paperwork and got myself on the delayed entry program. Delayed entry just meant I would not go to basic training for another month or so. During that month, I decided to go back to work for my stepfather. He had started a remodeling business and was doing pretty well. I figured I was an adult, and it was only a short time anyway, so why not? The first thing he proceeded to do was to tell me how dumb I was for going into the Army. My response was simple, "Oh well, too late now." My work with him only went on for a few weeks. We were at a customer's property. He had taken to drinking again and was drinking heavily. He relieved himself on the customer's lawn then proceeded to lie down and pass out on the lawn. I picked up my things, proceeded to the train station, and was on my way. I would not see him for many years after that.

First Time in the Army

I got to basic training in July of 1987. After a night in reception, we were jammed into a bus with a shit ton of gear and yelled at for the next eight weeks. The yelling, screaming. Push-ups, grass drills (hours of physically punishing exercises to teach a lesson), cleaning, more cleaning, twenty-second showers, and…oh yeah…more yelling, were pretty much constant. I have to say, though, it didn't bother me. I knew they were trained to do this and that none of it was personal. I had been yelled at for many years, but it was meant as punishment and torture. This was character building, so no big deal for me. I also quickly learned that if you did what you were told, did it quickly and quietly, and yelled "Yes, Drill Sergeant" a lot, they would normally not know your name, and that was good. If a drill sergeant knew your name, it was for one of two reasons. You were either an exceptional soldier, which rarely happened, or you were, as they would say, a knucklehead. Knuckleheads got to do a lot of push-ups and got a lot of extra screaming. It built character!

I made it through basic training and moved on to my next step, the US Army Element School of Music in Norfolk, Virginia. I spent six months there and other than formations, physical training, and (much less tough) drill sergeants, it was kind of like going to college. We had our evenings and weekends free, and as long as we got approval, we could go off base. It was a good time for me. I finished my time in Norfolk and moved on to my first unit. The United States Army Band of New York City. What a place for a twenty-one-year-old to land. The base was in Brooklyn, New York. I got there and quickly became the lead singer of our rock band. We traveled throughout the year to nearby states. We also had a side band that would play on the weekends, and I would play my primary instrument, the tuba, with the New York University orchestra. It was a good time.

I did not start to gamble my first time in the Army, but I did begin to do things that were out of character for me and would later manifest into my addiction. I borrowed money from my fellow soldiers. In particular, I borrowed quite a bit of money from one particular fellow soldier. I was trying to build a side business to set myself up for the future. Steve was kind enough to lend me a fair amount of money to help get my business up and running. Looking back, I have to say my heart was never truly into that business. I had to hustle about NYC, handing out cards to get people to call a number, then get them to sit down with me so I could recruit them to sell a product and recruit other people to do the same. It took a level of assertiveness I simply didn't have at the time. But I will admit I really liked the rush of people calling the number and the prospect of getting rich. I would just back down any time someone would have a concern or objection. I felt like I would be hurting their feelings if I pushed, and I remember what having my feelings hurt felt like, so I never pushed and never really got the business off the ground. The other thing I never did was pay Steve back, at least not until years later when his persistence and my first wife moved me to get him paid back. If it weren't for those two things, I honestly don't know if I would have paid him back.

Her Again

Just a brief diversion from the buildup of my gambling addiction. One day I was sitting in my barracks room at the post in New York. My phone rang. It actually took me back because my phone rarely rang. Most everyone I knew lived in the same building as me, so they would just knock on my door. I would call my mother more than she would call me. So when I heard the ring, I got curious and picked up. It was the woman I had dated my senior year in high school, the one I let go on my front steps in January of 1985. Here it was, about five years later, and she was calling me. We talked for a while, and I eventually invited her to New York. I got her a room at the guesthouse on the post. It wasn't long before we were again dating. She was fresh out of college and finding her way in the working world outside of Philadelphia. I was a young military musician stationed in New York City. It was a long-distance relationship, but it seemed to work for a while. Roughly a month and a half into our second time together, we were sitting at a bar and restaurant near my mother's place in Pennsylvania. She kindly told me that she had found someone else and wanted to see where it would go. She let me go. We had not gotten in too deep, so I was okay with it and understood. We also had not gone far enough that I would need to reveal the "deeper me," so I didn't know if I would have had the same resistance.

I very much enjoyed my time in New York. I got to sing often, and I joined a theater company and got to do some acting, which I always very much enjoy. Acting always allowed me to get outside of myself and go deeper because it wasn't me that was being exposed. I did get into another relationship while I was there. I met her through the theater company I was working with. She was quite striking and quite passionate. We had a whirlwind of a relationship that extended beyond me leaving the Army. I got an apartment in Brooklyn, and we would spend time at each other's place. But then it began to happen again. We were starting to get serious. She wanted to know more about me and where I grew up and about my family. I again got scared. It was Christmas time, and we had bought gifts for each other. But instead of sitting with a warm hot cocoa on Christmas Eve and exchanging kisses and gifts, I ran home to Pennsylvania. Shortly after that, my brother came back with me and helped move me out of that apartment. I never spoke with her again and I regret that. She deserved better.

Civilian Life, Marriage, and Children

I came back to Pennsylvania at the end of 1991. I spent a fair amount of time looking for work. During that time, my aunt came up to visit from Florida. We had a great visit, and I decided to drive her home. I had nothing to do, and it would give me a chance to get away for a bit. We got down to Florida, and it wasn't long before my cousins and uncle offered me a job. So I went back to Pennsylvania, grabbed my stuff, and headed back to Florida to live with my aunt and uncle and work in roofing and siding. That went well at first. But I have to say I didn't really enjoy the work. I also struggled with my cousin who lived in the same house and struggled with alcoholism. I loved my cousin, but I had a hard time being around him because he needed to drink daily. I was finding myself wanting to drink more and more, and I had promised myself I would never end up like my father or stepfather. I made the decision to move out and moved in with my grandmother and uncle who lived down the road. I also left my job and took a job selling advertising to military welcome guides. I had to call businesses around military bases to get them to buy ads. It again required an assertiveness I was not ready to give, and I didn't make much money doing it. I couldn't pay rent to my grandmother. At one point, she told my mother she thought I was a mooch and taking advantage of her. When I heard this, I immediately moved out, and for a short time, I lived homeless on the beaches of South Florida.

A guy I was working with said he was renting a house with some of his friends and asked if I wanted to join them. He was also an Army veteran so I said I would. I did need a place to live after all. I got to the house, and it was right out of a surfer movie. The house was in okay shape, but there was literally no furniture. Everyone lived on bedrolls on the floor. Everyone in the house lived on convenience store potato chips, beer, and weed. I cringed, but I needed a roof over my head, and this would do for now. During my stay at this house, my mother and brother came down for a visit with my aunt and uncle. We got another visitor during that time. It was Hurricane Andrew, which pretty much obliterated a huge swath of land south of where I was. We got minimal damage. Not long after all of that, I made the decision to go back to Pennsylvania.

It seemed I could never settle. I had moved around so much in my first twenty-four years it was staggering. I felt like a man without a home. I made it back to Pennsylvania and found the first real job I had since I was in the Army. I took a job as a technician with a lawn fertilization company. I had a residential route and would spread fertilizer, spray weeds, and recommend additional services. I liked working with the customers because the company I worked for believed in an informed approach. We told customers why something was happening and recommended a more natural approach. I started there in 1993, and by 1994, I was in a leadership role. I was an operational field coordinator. Not long after that, I became the branch manager. And not long after that, I would meet the woman who would become my first wife.

A Whirlwind

I met her in a bar. My brother and I had a two-man acoustic act and would play on the weekends. At the time he was dating someone, and the woman she was dating brought a friend along to this gig. I had not dated in a long time and was attracted to her, and pretty quickly, we were dating. She lived in a house not too far from where I was working. So, when my car broke down about a month into our relationship, she invited me to stay with her. I quickly accepted. Our relationship was more physical than anything early on. I didn't have to give much of myself, so I was enjoying it. Also, by now my mother had separated from and divorced my stepfather. He was out of the picture and no longer an influence in any of our lives. So I had no issue introducing her to the family. I have to say, early on my mother didn't really care for her. She felt like she was self-serving and too demanding of me. But I honestly didn't notice then. I was blinded by love. We ended up finding an apartment and moving in together, and that's when I began to realize that there more to her than I was ready to deal with.

Not long into living in our new apartment, she was talking about the boyfriend she had before dating me. They were together for many years, and he talked her into moving to the town she was living in when we met. Then he left her, and she was scarred. Unfortunately, I got to take the blame for all of the wrong he had done to her. I made attempts to explain to her that I wasn't him, but unfortunately, I got to be the poster child for all things wrong with the male species. I was seeing that she had some issues of her own to unravel. I stayed with her hoping things would get better. At the end of 1995, we got engaged, and we moved from our apartment into a house her mother owned. I was moving up in my company and working some pretty intense hours. Then one evening, she called and told me I had to come home immediately. I told her I was in the middle of something, but in her "never take no for an answer" way, she insisted. I went home. It was about an hour's drive. I was frustrated that she had made me drive all that way but wouldn't tell me what was going on. I got to the house. She was sitting in the middle of the living room floor. She didn't say anything. She just handed me something. I looked down. It took a few seconds, but then I realized I was looking at a pregnancy test, and it was positive.

My daughter was born in October of 1996. She was the shining star in my life and my reason for being. I wanted to work my ass off to make sure she would have the best life possible. But I was also fighting an inner battle. I was getting the growing sense that I just didn't have a desire to be married to my first wife anymore. She was, as I saw it, demanding. I felt like I was not allowed to be me. I had to be who she wanted me to be. In hindsight, I think I owned as much of that as she did. I never stepped up for myself. Even when I felt like I was right, I questioned myself. And I became passive-aggressive, holding my tongue until I couldn't take it anymore, then slamming doors and breaking things. I felt pressured at work too. She felt like I worked too many hours and didn't make enough money. It was getting out of hand. We went on a vacation, and I extended my vacation without saying anything. I wanted to keep her happy. I got fired for that. But there was more to it. I was not the go-getting employee I had once been. I felt defeated. I felt owned. I showed up to work and went through the motions, but not much more.

After being let go by that company, which I had worked at for more than five years, we moved again. I took a job delivering for a hardware store then took a job with an old employer. The son of the owner of the pizza shop I had worked at in high school opened his own restaurant and was looking for a manager. The fit was good, and I got the job. During this time, I found out I was going to be a father again. I felt I was in this marriage whether I wanted to be or not at this point. My hours were not great at work. I worked six days a week. I'd get there at eleven in the morning and leave anywhere between 2:00 AM and 4:00 AM. I hated being away from my daughter, but if I'm being honest, I didn't mind being away from my first wife. By this time, we did more arguing than anything. And I felt more like an employee than a husband. But I was a father and had another on the way. I couldn't do these hours forever. One day, on a whim, I asked my wife what she thought of the idea of me going back into the Army. I sold the idea by talking about free housing and medical care and the fact that my old job as a musician was a pretty safe one. She agreed to the idea, so I began the process of getting back into the Army.

A Retread

I did the paperwork to get back into the Army. At the time, I could not go back into the band field. They did not have openings. So I looked at my options and chose food inspector. It seemed like a field that would not see a lot of combat and could provide a career beyond the Army with the USDA or FDA or some other group. I was told I did not need to go back to basic training but that I would need to go to Fort Leonard Wood, Missouri, to get processed back in then onto Fort Sam Houston, Texas, to go to school for several weeks to learn how to do my job. While I was at these places, my wife and daughter would move in with my wife's grandmother and grandfather. They would move in with me when I got to my first duty station, in December of 1999, at Great Lakes Naval Center, north of Chicago.

My first wife and I both smoked when we met. When she got pregnant, she decided we needed to quit. She did. I kept smoking but kept it a secret. When she would tell me I smelled like smoke, I would say I work around smokers. It was easy to do because so many people smoked then. When I was away at Ft. Leonard Wood and Ft. Sam Houston, I took full advantage of my freedom and smoked more than I can say. No one was there to yell at me. It's strange looking back. I had developed a full-blown "you're not the boss of me" attitude, but I would never show that outwardly. I lived that in my own fantasy bubble that I had created for myself. My ego told me I was in control of everything. My reality painted a very different picture, and that created conflict within me. While I was at Fort Sam Houston, something amazing happened. I was in a class when the sergeant came in and said I had a phone call. My first instinct was to panic and wonder what was wrong because phone calls in the middle of class just didn't happen. I picked up the phone, and my wife told me I was father to a baby boy. You could not have brought me down off the high I felt that day if you had punched me in the gut. I was a dad again. I would have been as happy if I had a girl. But I had a son. Someone to carry on the name. That was one of the happiest days of my life. I made it through my training and got to Great Lakes in mid-December. I had not met my son yet. I went back to Pennsylvania and met him, and after the holidays, we all traveled out to Great Lakes together.

It was good to have my family back together. I started to get to know my son and reconnect with my daughter. It was also an opportunity to try to reset my relationship with my wife. We were in a new place, nowhere near home, and had a brand-new opportunity. I would say at first it worked, but over time, our connection began to erode again. There was a soldier stationed at a remote station in Wisconsin. He put out a request to swap, and we saw this as a good opportunity. So about midway through my first assignment, we again packed our bags and moved north to Fort McCoy in the dead middle of nowhere.

We bought a mobile home on a government plot in Wisconsin. It was nice to have our own home. I had taken a part-time job ton help us get ahead of the bills. We were making progress financially and growing as a family. But the relationship between my first wife and me was strained. We did not talk nearly as often as we once did. We were back to arguing. I felt throttled and trapped. I still smoked and hid my smoking. No one was going to tell me how to live my life, but I wasn't going to openly stand for myself either. Then I came down on orders to Korea. I would need to reenlist or extend my current enlistment to go to Korea. After a number of arguments and calm conversations, the decision was made that I would go to Korea. Then…September 11, 2001, came.

The Gambling Soldier

Korea

"No one is more professional than I. I am a noncommissioned officer, a leader of soldiers. As a noncommissioned officer, I realize that I am a member of a time-honored corps, which is known as the backbone of the Army…" That's the opening phrase of the Army creed of the noncommissioned officer. It holds us to a high standard and sets the bar for enlisted leadership in the Army. I used to live by that creed. Then came gambling.

When the events of September 11, 2001, took place, I was stationed at a National Guard post in the middle of Wisconsin. I was an active duty sergeant. There were a small number of us stationed there to fill in positions the National Guard couldn't. Mine, of course, was one of those positions. At that time, I was there with my first wife, my son, and my daughter. My children were both under the age of six. Earlier that year, I had come down on orders for an unaccompanied, one-year tour in the Republic of Korea. I considered leaving the Army since I would need to reenlist to go to Korea, and the thought of being away for a year was not overly appealing to me. But after several conversations with my first wife, some of them a bit heated, I made the decision to "raise my right hand" and go to Korea. Then…9/11.

The events that took place that September created quite a bit of stress. Now, my year separated from my family was going to be in a nation bordering a country the president was calling part of the "axis of evil." This didn't sit well with me, and it created more arguments between my ex and me. Now the prospect of leaving my children took on a whole new dimension. But I was committed. There was no turning back. Plus, I was a noncommissioned officer in the US Army. I was honor bound to fulfill my duty to my country. So on a cold day in November 2001, I boarded a plane that started my journey to Korea.

Roughly a day after I left the airport in Wisconsin, I arrived at Osan Air Base in the Republic of Korea. There was a twelve-hour time difference between Korea and home, and I had been on three planes and sleeping on my duffel bag in Seattle to get there. I was tired. My first indication that we had entered Korea during a tense time was the Patriot missiles that were pointed at the plane as we approached the runway, and the stranded barbed wire all around the base. Level up the tension. After deboarding the plane, we were taken through that hanger and, after some time, were loaded on buses. The next leg of the journey was to Seoul and Yongsan Base.

Yongsan is the central command facility for the Army in the Republic of Korea. It sits in then Yongsan District, or Dragon Hill district, pretty much smack in the center of Seoul. Everyone from my unit, and pretty much any soldier processing into Korea, started their journey at Yongsan before moving on to their final destination. So to Yongsan we went. We arrived in the evening and were brought to the Dragon Hill Lodge to be put up for the night before beginning our in-processing the next day. The Dragon Hill Lodge was a four-star hotel on an Army base. There are several of these throughout the world, and I was lucky enough to be put up in this one. We were offloaded, checked in to our rooms, and given our meeting times and places for the next morning. Then, we were on our own.

After throwing all of my stuff in my room, I ventured to the main lobby area. I was tired, but nowhere near ready to sleep because of my stress level. I missed my family already. I was settling into the realization that when I was back with my children, they would be a year older. I was playing the argument my wife, and I had in my head and regretting not having more time to settle anything. And, oh by the way, I was in a foreign country that was within striking distance of another, potentially hostile country. Sleep was not on my agenda. But food was. I was hungry. So, I ventured to the lobby. This hotel had a couple of very good restaurants, along with some quick stops for food. It was like a small mall or plaza. I don't remember exactly what I had, just that it was quick and easy. I then began to roam through this wonderland to see what was there. As I was walking around, I came across a room. This wasn't a conference room or restaurant. This was a casino-style slot machine room. It was very small compared to a full casino, but big enough to look like one.

I grew up in eastern Pennsylvania, not too far from Atlantic City. In the years before legal gambling became widespread in the states, Atlantic City was the place to go for those of us who wanted to have a little fun. I gambled in AC when I was younger. I was able to take a specific amount of money with me, and either leave when it was gone or leave with some money in my pocket. So when I saw this slot room at the Dragon Hill Lodge, I thought it could be a good way to kill some time until I felt like I could sleep. So I took about a hundred bucks out of the ATM, and off I went.

Danger, Danger

After roaming around the slot room for a while, I found what looked like an interesting machine to sit in front of. It was digital and had little race cars that dropped into boxes. I believe there were nine total. The idea was to get a straight or diagonal line of cars or to fill the screen with cars. It was also touchscreen, so I could touch each box independently and stop it midspin. So why not? I dropped a twenty into the machine and off I went. It felt good to take my mind off the anxiety I had been going through for a bit. I still felt the pressures of the day, and the weeks leading up to my departure, but at least I wasn't in the middle of having to do something, and I could sit mindlessly, at least for a bit.

Then, it happened. I was randomly touching the boxes to stop them. Car...car...car...car...car...car. Everything lit up. Music started to play. Littles cars started dancing all over the screen, and the payout line began to roll upward. I couldn't tell you exactly how much I won. I didn't break the bank, but it was in the hundreds, for sure. I can tell you that, in that moment, as the cars lined up and the music started playing and the dollar amount rose, all the fear and anger and anxiety and stress I was feeling washed away. And for a short time, things felt really good!

I obviously didn't know this at the time but very often a win is what begins to trigger the compulsion to gamble more, which can and often does lead to addictive behaviors. I won't say a magical switch was flipped, and I suddenly became an addicted gambler, but I will say that I believe that was the night it began. That feeling was good. Maybe more appropriately, those bad feelings weren't there. I liked the excitement. I liked the good feeling. But I think I mostly liked the stress not being there. These were feelings I simply did not want to deal with, and I basically spent my life finding ways to avoid feelings I didn't want to deal with, and this way seemed pretty cool at the time.

I made it through that night and through all of the orientations, classes, and paperwork I needed to complete. Two days after getting to Yongsan, I was picked up by my new team and taken four hours south to my new home for the next year, Camp Hialeah in Pusan… or Busan depending on who you are. This was at the southern end of the Korean peninsula, right off the Pacific Ocean. It was a small, quiet post in a big city. I arrived and was moved into a house on the base with three other noncommissioned officers from different units. I was in a unit leadership role and was treated accordingly. Over the next few days, I settled into my new home and my new role. I met the outgoing noncommissioned officer in charge (NCOIC) and began the transition process. As a side note, I quickly discovered how poor the air quality is in Korea when we conducted physical training, and I quite literally couldn't breathe in the middle of a run. I came to find out later this was called the "Korean crud," an upper respiratory infection most people who are new to the country go through as they adjust to the air quality.

It took me a good week or so to begin to get into a rhythm and learn the base. On my first weekend, the outgoing NCOIC took a bunch of us to the community club, the base bar, as part of her fare-well tour. While we were at the club, I noticed a small room off to the side of the club. Curious, I strolled over and took a look. Sure enough, it was a casino-style slot room. This one was much smaller and more rustic than the one in Seoul but still held several machines, including the car-popping game I played and won on while at Yongsan. I didn't play that night but kept it in mind for another day. Another day came the next day, Saturday.

Weekends were boring in Korea, at least for me. I was alone and without my family. I really didn't know anyone, and it was a small base. So, my first Saturday there I wandered into the slot room. It was probably around 10:00 AM that I walked in. I just wanted to check it out. I again took about a hundred dollars from the ATM and sat down at the car game. I didn't win anything that day, but the memory of what happened in Seoul stuck with me, and I think that kept me there trying. Eventually, I left that machine and moved to a more traditional one-armed bandit. I started winning again. They were small wins, but they kept me playing. And I was beginning to notice that these small wins, and the ability to extend my play time gave me the same sense of relief from stress and anxiety I got from the win. Plus, it was keeping the boredom away.

This pattern developed gradually, with visits on a Saturday, which then became visits on a Friday and eventually Sunday. We would occasionally take the train to Taegu, the next town and base north of us. We had a small contingent there, which I was also in charge of. While there, I discovered two more, even smaller slot rooms. I would also take the four-hour train into Seoul on long weekends and visit the room at the Dragon Hill Lodge. My stress distraction was now beginning to develop into a habit. I felt like that was my escape from boredom and my go-to on the weekends. Yes, I'd go to the club or take part in the Hasher club. Hashing was a running game with a drinking element. It would take forever to describe it. Suffice to say, it was called a drinking game for people with a running problem. But mostly, I would hit the rooms.

As my time in Korea went on, my desire to gamble became stronger. Of course, most of the time was consumed with day-to-day operations, planning for field exercises, going to field exercises, etc. But there was also a fair amount of downtime, and I found myself filling most of that downtime living in the slot rooms. The only problem was that the money was not keeping up with the need to gamble. While I was gambling much more frequently, more often than not I was walking out with nothing. This was a problem for me because as my need to gamble was growing, so was the amount with which I was gambling. Where thirty, fifty, or one hundred bucks got me through early on, that amount no longer provided the same relief because I was now betting in higher amounts to get the same thrill and to "chase the big win." This presented a dilemma for me because the need was growing, but what I had to spend wasn't. So began the downfall.

Because my drive to gamble was getting more intense, and the amount I needed to play to get the same thrill was growing, I started to do things that were out of character for me. My first wife would put a set amount of money into my account each month. I began to give her reasons I needed more money. We were going on a trip. I had a soldier who needed help. My bike needed repair. I would tell her whatever I could to get her to send more money. At first, she did. Then I got nervous because there were only so many times I could tell the same stories, and I knew she was getting close to questioning me. On to the next level I went. I sold my ten-speed bike I brought with me. I was getting me around, but since the only places I ever went were work and the game room, and since I needed money fast, I sold it. I sold a small TV-DVD combo I brought with me. I sold my CD player. I sold almost everything I wasn't wearing on my back. For a short time, this worked. But I eventually ran out of stuff. By then, it was time for my midtour leave.

Midtour

Midtour leave was a thirty-day vacation back home. It was a chance for me to get out of Korea and see my family and, hopefully, shrug this growing need to gamble. I can tell you I did not gamble the entire time I was home. I did get some urges, but I was able to shrug them because I was so happy to be with my children and because I really didn't want my first wife knowing what I had done. I felt ashamed that I had allowed myself to go that far. But I can also remember thoughts coming up of how to get money to take back with me. Those thoughts weren't all-consuming then, but they were there. I can remember getting projects done around the house and going places with the family and seeing family back home in Pennsylvania. It felt normal and I enjoyed it. I also knew it was thirty days and that I would be going back.

As my leave drew nearer to its end, I can remember a couple of different feelings. I can remember feeling sad that I was again leaving my family for another six months. I can remember feeling stressed about going back to a place and environment I really didn't want to be in. But I can also remember feelings of excitement and anticipation because I would be going back to my "happy place," and no one was there to monitor me. By no one, of course I mean my ex. Those feelings created more anxiety for me because I didn't want to go back to the rooms. I wanted that behind me and thought I'd done a pretty good job of shrugging it off while I was home. But as I later learned, addiction doesn't work that way.

Back to the ROK

It was summer, and I was back in the Republic of Korea or ROK as they called it. I jumped right back into my work. Before I left for mid-tour, I had accomplished two pretty major things. First, I went on an intensive two-week exercise to earn the Army's expert field medical badge or EFMB. This is a badge that is incredibly hard to earn. I was told, at the time, it only has about a 16 percent completion rate. I don't think that's changed much. I met medics there who were on their fifth, sixth, eighth, and ninth tries. I'm not quite sure how, but I earned it on my first try. The other big thing that happened is that I got promoted from sergeant to staff sergeant. That was a promotion for which I worked very hard and of which I was extremely proud. These things were happening while my need to gamble was growing. I began to feel a bit like Dr. Jekyll and Mr. Hyde. One side of me was accomplishing great things for my career while the other was going down a darkening path. Neither side was winning.

So, I got back to the ROK in the summer and went right back to work. I had field exercises to prepare for, reviews to do, new soldiers to orient, and ever-present leadership meetings. For a short time, gambling was not on that to-do list. But it didn't take long for me to start to venture back into the rooms again, and when I did the dive back down, the "rabbit hole" happened very quickly. There was not a gradual buildup to where I had left off. Once I started again, my desire level basically picked up where I left off and grew pretty damn quickly. It wasn't too long before the money I had couldn't keep up with the desire I had. I had already sold everything I had, and the flow from home was not an option. What I did next still has my head spinning to this day. I began to borrow from my sub-ordinates. I would give them crazy excuses as to why I needed the money, like "there's a problem with my bank," "I'm fighting with my wife and she cut me off," and others. Right from the start, I could feel their hesitance and discomfort, but they did it anyway. By the way, for a noncommissioned officer in the Army to do what I did is already inexcusable. That level of leadership is about being there for subordinates and leading by example and being the rock for younger soldiers to lean on and learn from. At that time, I was none of these things. I regret even as I'm writing this. Eventually, they very kindly started to say no. It was something that needed to happen, although at the time you couldn't convince me of that.

So here I was. I was now beyond need. I had reached the point of full obsession. I had to go to the slot rooms whenever I could. I went every night of the week. I went on my lunch breaks. I started to make up leadership meetings I had to attend so I could sneak away and gamble. Couple this with ever-shrinking access to money. I smoked at the time. I would not buy cigarettes; instead, I would walk around the base with a bag. I would go to all of the outdoor, sand ashtrays and pick out all of the half-smoked butts from them. I knew this was a health risk, but I didn't care. As much as I needed to smoke, I needed to gamble even more. Anyway, like I was saying, couple my ever-growing need to gamble with ever-shrinking access to money, and I stepped into the unthinkable.

It was nighttime. I was at my quarters, lying in bed, obsessing over the fact that I had no money, and it would be some time before I would have access to more. I was scheming, desperately trying to figure out a way to gamble, and the thought occurred. We had cash at the unit to fund the veterinary clinic that was part of our operation. I knew it was there. I had access to it, and in my mind, I would win it back and put it back before anyone knew what happened. I say "in my mind." What I mean by that is I had convinced myself I could put the money back to justify the incredibly illegal thing I was about to do, knowing full well that I had a fifty-fifty shot, at best of returning that money. In fact, I was more likely to gamble until it was all gone than anything. Again, Dr. Jekyll knows this is wrong and the result will not be good. Mr. Hyde is convinced it's no big deal, and gambling was more important than anything. Risk be damned.

Please understand, I am a caring person who really does want to do right by others, by my family, by my job and coworkers. But in that moment, for what was probably the first time, I was ready to put all of that aside to feed my obsession. It was not long until my decision was made, and I stole the money.

Trouble

Naturally, it wasn't long after I took the money, and couldn't put it back, that someone noticed it was missing. Once that happened, things began to move quickly. My unit officer in charge quickly contacted the base police and criminal investigation division (CID) because, even though it wasn't a tremendous amount of money, someone had indeed stolen money and it needed to be investigated. They began to look through the facility and fingerprint everything and interview my soldiers. I knew my fingerprints would have already been on everything because I was the NCOIC. I also knew I wasn't willing to allow my squad to go through a lengthy investigation, and I was swimming in shame at this point. I was a noncommissioned officer. I was supposed to be above all of this. So I turned myself in and confessed.

I don't remember all of the exact details of my interview with CID. I remember it being pretty long, and I remember both being a train wreck and feeling a sense of relief at the same time. No matter what the outcome, I would be free of this freaky obsession I had with these rooms. I couldn't go back at this point. I was done for good! At least that's what I thought at the time. So the investigation was over, and I was sent back to my quarters to await my fate. I was nearing the end of my tour, so I knew no matter what, I'd be leaving Korea soon. I just had no clue whether that would be as a soldier, a civilian, or a resident of Ft. Leavenworth where the Army's prison is located. So, I sat in my quarters, and I waited.

I can remember a leader in my unit (I think it was my first sergeant) asking if I needed someone to check in on me. Frankly, that confused me, so I asked why I would need that. The answer was that I seemed distraught, and they wanted to make sure I wasn't going to hurt myself. I'm not gonna lie. I can't say those thoughts didn't come up, but I didn't feel like I was going to do anything about them. Plus, if I was going to do something, would I really have said yes when I was asked? Looking back, that shows a very clear lack of understanding of what I was going through. In any case, I said no… and I waited.

I was told to get all of my things together because I was being moved to our headquarters in Seoul on Yongsan base. This is where it all began, and apparently, this is where my fate was to be decided. So, pack I did, and to Seoul I went. I was put up in enlisted barracks. I had to live among soldiers who knew I was leaving in shame. I was there for a couple of weeks, as I recall, and it was lonely.

A few days after my arrival, I finally met with my unit commander. He was an even-tempered and very intelligent colonel with many years of service under his belt and a soldier-first approach to his job. But he could also be tough. When he started a sentence with "What I'd like to see is…" it meant "get it done, no excuses." I was admittedly more nervous than I probably was my entire time in Korea. It wasn't too many months before that meeting that the colonel was praising the work I and other NCOs had done to improve the training quality in the unit. Now, here I sat, embarrassed and ashamed because I allowed this ridiculous obsession to get the better of me.

My commander was very calm in our meeting but also very direct. He made it clear that my actions were not acceptable, which I did not argue, and that I was to immediately be reduced in rank from staff sergeant to sergeant. I would also remain in the barracks at Yongsan and perform random duties, as assigned, until my departure date later that month. I also had to meet with my first sergeant to get my final NCO evaluation for my year on the peninsula. I received top or nearly top marks in every category but one, which I believe had something to do with character. Here is where my indiscretions were brought up, and again, I had to face the embarrassment head-on. I had the highest level of respect for my first sergeant. To listen to her describe her disappointment was extremely tough for me. But it needed to happen.

After these meetings were done, I was sent to the admin area to help organize files or something similar. I can remember sitting there and processing what had just happened. I remember the feelings of guilt and shame and embarrassment. I also remember feeling grateful and frankly a bit confused that the punishment was as light as it was. I had lied to subordinates and my unit officer. I stole money from my unit. I left during work hours to gamble. Yet I was leaving with a reduction of one rank and a black mark on my record. That was it. The other thing that confused me was that no one attempted to try to understand what I was going through. I didn't see any counselors. I was sent to one clergy member while I was still in Pusan. He simply suggested I go to bingo night to pass the time. Bingo night?

The process of getting ready to leave Korea had begun. I started visiting different offices to out process and in between these visits I would clean barracks or file paperwork. What I did not do was tell my first wife what was happening. As far as she knew, I was leaving on time. The adjustment in pay hadn't taken effect yet and wouldn't until I left. So I had time to craft my excuse for the "pay mistake." I was flying home to Wisconsin, and immediately moving on to South Carolina, and my next unit. But my wife and children were staying in Wisconsin until the following June so my kids could finish their school year. So I would not have to "face her." That's right! I had stopped going to the game rooms. I had gotten myself in trouble. But I was nowhere near recovery.

Back in the USA

In late November of 2002, I was back in the United States after one of the most bizarre years of my life in Korea. I was glad to be home. I missed my family. But I carried quite a bit of baggage back with me. I lost rank. I had a black mark on my otherwise stellar record. My first wife had no clue about any of this, and I had a growing addiction that would manifest in ways I couldn't have imagined at the time. But in late November of 2002, none of that mattered. I was home.

I spent the next couple of weeks at home. I was able to reconnect with my kids and wife. I honestly don't remember how I lied my way through the reduction in pay, but I did. I was also able to do some work around the house. On top of all of this, my first wife got me a pickup truck. I had always wanted a truck. It was a small one, a Ford Ranger, but I didn't care. I had a truck. I did not gamble or even think about gambling while I was home in Wisconsin. The holidays, time with family, and preparing for my move south kept me preoccupied. So by the time I left for South Carolina, I was feeling like myself again, despite the stress of leaving my family again.

Before the end of 2002, I loaded the truck, said goodbye (for now) to my family, and began the journey toward South Carolina. It was a couple days of driving to get where I was going, and by the end of my first day of driving, I had made it to Kentucky. I was finding somewhere to stop for the night when I noticed a sign—a sign for a casino. I was thinking it was early, and I had made good time. I was also feeling pretty good and felt like what I had experienced in Korea was behind me. So...again...I decided to stop for a bit. Well, a bit turned into several hours. I did leave with money, but I also left with the urge to play more.

The next day, I made it into South Carolina. I was not going to be stationed on a military base. Instead, I'd be living in the community and my work site was at a factory that packaged meals, ready to eat or, as they're more commonly known, MREs. I was to be a quality inspector at the plant. So when I got to Mullins, South Carolina, I spent my first few weeks in a hotel. This hotel was one of those where contractors stayed, and things happened that I really didn't care to know about. I went into work for my first day. The team I was going to work with was really nice. The noncommissioned officer in charge knew about what happened in Korea, but he did not make a big deal out of it, and if any of my other coworkers knew anything, I never knew it. I made the rounds, met everyone, got oriented into my job, and to work I went. There was not a casino anywhere near me. In fact, the closest one at the time was six hours away, so I felt safe from my new habit.

It didn't take long until my new job and my new town began to feel lonely. I missed my family. My new coworkers all had families they went home to every day. I didn't know anyone in the area and then locals didn't seem overly interested in being friendly. I watched TV, but there was only so much to watch. I called home periodically, which was far easier than in Korea since I was only one time zone away. I did eventually move out of the hotel and into a very small but quiet apartment in the area. I was glad to be away from the hotel, but I was also getting more lonely and more bored by the day. At the time, I smoked, so I stopped by a convenience store one day to pick up some cigarettes and happened to see the scratch-off lottery tickets behind the counter. I had seen these for years at home and really didn't give them a second thought. Now it seemed like something to have a moment of fun with, so I bought some, and so began my second obsession.

Scratching

Not too long into my assignment in South Carolina I began to play scratch-off lottery tickets. Since there were no casinos nearby, and online gambling was not close to being a thing yet, this seemed a good alternative and seemed to satisfy my cravings. I again started off with small amounts. I would buy a five-dollar ticket here or a handful of dollar tickets there. But just like the slots in Korea, the amount I was spending on lottery began to grow. The games I would play changed too. I went from very simple "match three symbols, win a prize" to the longer playing bingo and crossword games. These games excited me more because the anticipation of winning as I revealed more numbers or letters was every bit as energizing as winning a prize. It's what I discovered later to be known as a near win. It's also why I got excited playing slot machines. Getting close to the win, before the game was even complete, created excitement, which put me in a space where the world around me didn't exist. So my addiction again took off, and it took off quickly. At first, my wins were enough to keep me going. But just like the machines overseas, eventually losing, or the sheer amount of time I was playing, caught up with me and the need for money was more than the amount of money I had. My old ways of getting money were no longer available. I couldn't borrow from my coworkers. I couldn't ask the wife for more. And there was no way in hell I was stealing again (so I thought…more about that later), so I needed a new source. I would discover that new source, and a new danger soon, but first…my first trouble.

I was stationed in South Carolina, basically just south and east of the North Carolina border and about a half an hour from Interstate 95, which is the main road leading from Maine to Florida.

My mother lived in Pennsylvania, which was about a ten-hour drive up the road. So I decided to make an impromptu trip home to visit Mom. To be honest, yes, I wanted to see my mother, but what I really wanted was to get some money from her so I could continue to feed my habit. I did not make the wisest choices during my addiction. Okay, I made really ridiculous, dumb choices during my addiction. I was in the Army. If I wanted to travel more than about fifty miles from where I was, I had to have permission from my unit. I did not ask for permission. It was a long weekend, and I figured I could make it there and back in no time. My wife and kids were in Wisconsin, and the rest of my team was at home with their families. So what was the big deal, right?

I took off in the morning on my journey north. It was raining in South Carolina. It was a light rain, but pretty warm, so no problem. I drove into and through North Carolina, which took a couple of hours. As I was driving north, the temperature was dropping, but I still wasn't concerned because it was rain. Now, logical, clear-thinking me would have thought, *I'm going north. It's going to get colder, not warmer. Maybe I should wait.* Actually, logical, clear-thinking me would have never made the trip in the first place, at least not without clearing it. But this was not logical, clear-thinking me. This was "becoming more obsessed by the day" me. So I kept driving north. I reached the border and crossed into Virginia. As I did, I began to notice the ice forming on the trees and the side of the road. At that point, logic began to take over, and I convinced myself to turn around at the next exit and head back. No sooner had that thought entered my mind, and I hit an overpass. This was a pretty long overpass. My first thought was those signs you see that say, "Bridge freezes before road," so I began to slow down. A tractor trailer was in the other lane so it could pass me when it caught up, but it never made it that far. Midway across the overpass, I began to slide. Now, I grew up in the northeast part of the country, so I knew what to do. I took my foot off the gas and gently turned into the slide. Nothing! I continued to slide, and it was getting worse. The tractor trailer was still creeping up on me. As I approached the end of the overpass, I went into a tailspin. I spun around and was directly facing the big rig just as it reached me. It hit me. It hit me head-on and pushed the entire cab in six inches. I went flying into the grass median between the north- and south-bound lanes. I'm really grateful that median was there because it immediately slowed me down, and it kept me from sliding into oncoming traffic. I slid to a stop.

I just sat there for a minute. The impact was so hard it blew out the side windows and pushed the dashboard up to my knees, but I didn't seem to be hurt. I searched around for my phone, which had been sitting on the seat next to me. It had fallen on the floor. I picked it up and pushed my way out of the truck. I wanted to check on the tractor trailer driver. He was a few hundred feet away, parked on the shoulder. He had a minor dent to his fender, and he was fine. He had radioed the accident, and the police were already on their way. In the meantime, I gave him my insurance info, and he took off. I was glad he was alright. The police came. They took my information, assessed the truck, which was a total loss, and called a tow truck. The tow truck took me and my mangled Ranger to the next exit, which was only about a half a mile down the road.

The auto shop my truck was taken to had a mini market right next to it. I went in to figure out my next move. You see, I had no money. That's right, I had no money. I had spent it all on scratch-off tickets, which is why I was driving to Mom's in the first place. I was hungry and cold. I did happen to have an old checkbook in my truck. This checkbook was attached to an account I no longer used. I took a chance and wrote a check for some cigarettes, snacks, coffee, and a few bucks. They took it. This was before the days of electronic clearance, so I knew I had a shot. This was also quite dangerous because the Army would often counsel and punish soldiers for bouncing checks. But at the time, I didn't care. After getting warmed up and grabbing a smoke, I called my wife. I told her I had been in an accident. She was mad that I had even tried to make the trip. I hadn't told her about it. But she was glad that I was okay. I told her I had a ride back to Mullins. That was a lie. We hung up and I asked where the nearest truck stop was. I was told it was the next exit south. So I walked in the freezing rain for two miles to the truck stop. When I got there, I began to ask if anyone was headed south. After about a half hour I found a truck driver headed in my direction. He said he could take me as far as south of the border. This was a truck stop, tourist trap, gift shop, mini golf oasis just across the border in South Carolina. It was also about forty minutes from where I needed to be. I gratefully accepted his ride, being careful not to talk about money because, well, I didn't have any. He gave me the ride to south of the border. I then called my noncommissioned officer in charge (NCOIC) to see if he could pick me up and take me the rest of the way. He agreed but was not happy, and when I explained what had happened on the ride back, he was even less happy. I didn't get into trouble that day, but I could have, and I did get a pretty stern warning.

Not long after getting back, I got another car. My gambling urges were then put on hold. This was because we were in the midst of a national anthrax scare, and our hours had been increased by a lot. A group of reservists were brought in, and we went to two twelve-hour shifts, six days a week. I was put in charge of the night crew, which consisted of me and most of the reserve team. For the next few months, it was pretty much nothing but work and the few hours of sleep I could muster between. I don't sleep working overnight, so I got three to four hours a day and spent the rest of the time attempting to sleep. I had no desire to gamble.

The overnight shifts eventually ended. The reservists went home, and it was getting closer to summer. I had to find a house for my family, who would be down to join me soon. I was very excited by this and began looking immediately. I found a small house, across from a church in Marion, the next town over. It was time to be home again.

Back with Family, Finally

After a year in Korea, and about seven months in South Carolina, I was finally reunited with my family. They moved down in June of 2003. It was admittedly awkward at first. We had not lived as a family for over a year and a half. My children had grown. My first wife had to take on the role of both mom and dad. I also had some adjusting to do. I had become accustomed to living alone. It took a month or so, but we settled in and started acting like a family again. During this time, I was not gambling. I was so busy working and settling into our new home and lives that it barely crossed my mind. Looking back, I think that was a clue I could have paid attention to. When I was busy, and happy, my urges to gamble were less. I suppose hindsight really is twenty-twenty, isn't it?

Once the readjustment phase was over, and we were settled in, I found myself grabbing some scratch-off lottery tickets every now and then. We moved to a town about fifteen minutes from my office, and there were a couple of mini markets in between. So when I would stop to get gas or grab a pack of smokes, another habit I hid from my family, I'd pick up some lottery tickets and play them in the parking lot at work before going in. The urges weren't strong at first. It was just something to do. But they did get stronger as time went on, and eventually, I again found myself stopping on a daily basis and spending increasing amounts of money, again. As this got continuously worse, I found myself again needing more money. I found that money doing side jobs for the owners of the house we were living in at first. They bought old properties, and I would do mostly painting or cleanup work. I would tell my wife it was to make holiday gift money or get ahead on the bills or some other bullshit, but it was to gamble. After all, in my mind, I would win all of that money, so why worry about if I actually had it.

I took a job at a restaurant a few nights a week to make extra money. The paint jobs were slowing down, and I needed a cash flow. I have to be honest, I don't remember why this didn't become a major issue between my first wife and me at first. I was working a few days a week, and she wasn't really seeing anything from it. If I'm really being honest, I'm getting into some of the hazier times in my life. I'll recount the details as best I remember them, but I think I blacked out quite a bit. I was getting ready to head into some very dark years. It's uncomfortable for me to relive these years and necessary.

Several months after moving into our first house, we needed to find another one. There was something being done to the one we were in. Fortunately, the owner of the restaurant I was working at had a close friend who was renting a house. The house was big with a large garage, carport, and spacious yard. It was perfect. So again, we moved. During this entire time, my need to gamble was getting worse. I was working more hours and scratching more feverishly. I put in an application at one of the small loan places in town. I didn't expect much, but thought I would give it a shot. Sure enough, they approved me for about a thousand dollars. I had my cash. Around the same time, my wife took the children back to Pennsylvania to visit family. School was out, and she wanted to spend a couple of weeks with her mother and grandparents. I didn't have the leave time available, so I stayed.

The very first weekend my family was away, impulse took over. I found a casino at the other end of the state, about five hours away. I decided to head there early on a Saturday morning with my newly acquired loan money. I had about half of it or about five hundred bucks left. In my mind, I could spend the day, clean up, pay back the loan, and have some cash to spare. In case you haven't noticed by now, my mind was spinning some pretty tall tales to get me to gamble. This addiction is cunning. Anyway, I took off Saturday morning and got there about midday. I walked in and there was a giant building filled with the machines I loved so much in Korea. I did not start small and gradually increase my bets like I did when I first got to Korea. I went straight to quarter machines and straight to max bet. By the way, I was once again outside of the radius I could travel without approval. So I dove in and started playing, and it did not take long for me to run out of money. I was only there about two hours when I found myself dead broke and five hours from home. Fortunately, I had gassed up the car. So what did I do? I drove five hours home, took a couple hundred out of our vacation savings, and drove five hours back to that casino. In my mind, I had to. There was no way I could get wiped out that quickly! I had to win it back. I came to learn later this is called chasing losses. I would call it an all-consuming obsession! It compelled me and I saw no other options. I made that five-hour trip back across the state, marched into that casino, and lost all of that money I had just stolen from myself and my family. Again, I had gas in the car. I was able to make it back. Like I said, there is a lot about that time in my life I don't remember, but I very clearly remember the feelings of shame and guilt and hurt and anger I felt on that drive. How could I do that? How could I just take money from our family with *no* thought of what would happen? That was one of many trips I would take over the next several years with that feeling.

Make It Hurt

Over the next few months, my gambling addiction continued to grow. My lies got more creative. I spent less time with my children, and when I was with them, I wasn't really present. I began to feel like there was no way out of this mess. I couldn't tell anyone because I had already screwed up in Korea and didn't want to jeopardize my career. Plus, no one could possibly understand what was happening to me. I was losing it. I was so obsessed. I was becoming willing to do almost anything, but I knew I couldn't. It reached a point where I felt so lost, and I took a bunch of pills out of a bottle of pain pills I had for my bad back. I wanted it over. I was done, and no one would miss me or care once they found out what I had done. That's what I thought. I took the pills at work, and the next thing I remember was lying in an ambulance on the way to the hospital. I woke up more at the hospital. My boss was there, and not long after that, my wife showed up. I was in a haze. I had taken a handful of narcotic pain-killers. Apparently, my heart slowed down quite a bit, but it never stopped. I was hoping to fall asleep and not wake up. Well, I got the "fall asleep part" right. They kept me in the hospital until I was awake and alert enough to leave. Then my wife took me home. All I remember about the rest of that day was sitting on my back porch and crying uncontrollably for about fifteen minutes or so. This was my first attempt on my life.

My unit's reaction to my trip to the hospital was to ask if I was okay and tell me to go find a counselor. We weren't on a military base. We were about two hours away from the nearest one. So I had to find a civilian counselor. We found one about a half hour away and began to see her on a weekly basis. My wife went with me. She would talk about how her life was bad because I wouldn't "fix" myself, even though she really didn't have the slightest clue what needed to be "fixed." I would tell the counselor sad stories about my childhood, so she had something to write. I could recount traumatic memories and tell the story while remaining completely detached from the feelings that went with them. But I could look like I was feeling them. I could get through the hour without having to reveal what was really happening, which I couldn't begin to understand myself but felt I couldn't talk about it in front of my wife. This went on for a month or two. She finally seemed to feel we were on the right track, and we stopped meeting. I was done with the counseling and the weekly blame sessions from my wife. I don't remember anyone in my unit following up with me, and I have no clue if they followed up with the counselor. I was being left alone and that's what I wanted.

I continued to gamble. I kept it quiet after the incident, but still did it. I started taking out more small loans, and now had loan companies calling me because I wasn't making payments on time. I used a PO box and my cell number so none of this would ever get to the house. At one point, I had just gotten and spent a loan and was waiting for another. I was so desperate to gamble I raided my children's piggy banks and took all of the money they had in there. I also wrote a check from the investment account we had and cashed it at the restaurant where I worked. I'm sure the restaurant owner was concerned, or at least curious, but he never said anything and that's the way I wanted it.

Fort Sam Houston

During my assignment in South Carolina, I was selected to attend a basic leadership course, for noncommissioned officers, at Ft. Sam Houston in San Antonio, Texas. This school was a couple months long, and I would again be away from my family. I again packed up the car and headed south. On my way, I found a small casino in Alabama. I, of course, stopped. I couldn't stay long because I was on a time schedule. I also stopped overnight in Baton Rouge, Louisiana. It was just about right for an overnight stop, and there were multiple casinos to choose from. I did not get a lot of sleep that night, and I think I may have broken even. The next day, I finished the trip to San Antonio.

I was assigned my own room at Ft. Sam. Many of my fellow NCOs had roommates. In hindsight, that would have probably been a good thing. But I got a room by myself. The course was divided into two parts. The first part was general, so all different medical job skills were part of the class, and we focused on leadership skills and regulations. We had many classes focusing on the duties and requirements of a noncommissioned officer at a higher leadership level. We also did field exercises and got to act as squad leaders. The second part of the course was specific to my job skill. We did our physical training and went to morning formation with everyone then split off into our respective MOSs (jobs). During both phases of this course, I was gambling. There were no casinos in Texas, but the scratch-off lottery was as present in Texas as it was in South Carolina. I spent most, if not almost all, of my evenings and weekends running to different convenience stores to get lottery. I couldn't get loans, and there was no way I was borrowing in that environment. But I was among a handful of people who brought cars, so I'd give rides for gas money.

If I had no money, I'd go downtown and play free bingo at the USO in San Antonio. This is still one of my favorite cities, despite some bad experiences there. Two of my fellow NCOs became friends, and I would go to their room to watch movies on their laptop. That's when I wasn't gambling. I introduced them to my wife. I did this partly because I wanted her to meet my friends, but mostly because they provided me with an alibi when I wasn't calling home. She knew something wasn't right. She knew I wasn't right. I always denied it. She even got my new friends involved and had them talk with me. That just made me angry. I became more distant, and by the time I left San Antonio, I just didn't really want to be around her anymore. I wanted my own space so I could do what I wanted to do, which was gamble.

Separation

After getting back home to Marion, things were never the same. My ex and I argued more than we talked, but I don't remember the topic of the arguments. It was probably because she was trying to get me to explain why I was becoming so distant, and what was happening to all of our money, but I wanted nothing to do with that conversation. I just knew if I went down that rabbit hole there was no coming back, and by now, gambling had become my new best friend. It was that old, reliable buddy I could count on when the shit hit the fan or I was fighting or I felt sad or any time I just didn't want to deal with life. I was fully immersed in my obsession to gamble and didn't want to get out. So when I came down on orders to go back to Texas, this time it would be a permanent move to Corpus Christi, and the Naval Air Station there, my wife told me it was time for a talk.

My first wife made it clear to me that we were not the couple we were when we got married. I couldn't argue with that. She also said I was different when I got back from Korea. She wondered what had happened to me. There was no way I was going to tell her about my gambling experiences there, so I told her it was a very intense and stressful year. That, by the way, is not a lie. It was intense. It was stressful. But the trouble I caused and got into played a huge role in my being different. I was vague when we talked about it. I was also just generally distant. We went back and forth for a few weeks about what to do for this move. She finally decided she wanted to stay in South Carolina to give me a chance to get my head on straight. In essence, she wanted to separate, without legally separating. I didn't fight that because I still wanted her and the kids to get the benefits of being a military family, such as medical and housing allowance. I also convinced myself I could "fix this," and we could rebuild our lives.

But behind that was a sense of excitement. I was finally on my own. I could go and get this gambling thing out of my system once and for all. In the summer of 2004, I left for Texas again.

South Texas, End of the Road

Before I could go to Texas, I had to stop in Kentucky at Fort Campbell. This was the home of the headquarters for the region I was about to work in, so I needed to go meet the regional command. When I got there, the names had been released for the following month's promotion list. Amazingly, I made the list and had regained the rank I lost in Korea. I was very happy about this as it would allow me to live in South Texas and better take care of my family in South Carolina. I left control of the checking account with my first wife and told her I'd set up an account with a local bank and have her deposit a set amount each paycheck. She agreed to this and was probably relieved that I offered. I also knew that the money I had was mine. I could do with it whatever I wanted. I spent a day in Kentucky then off to Texas I went.

I was originally set to man a remote site about a half hour away from the detachment at Naval Air Station (NAS) Corpus Christi. But because of my promotion, I was kept at the NAS and was once again in the position of being the noncommissioned officer in charge. Because I was married and because of my position, I would not be allowed to get a room on base. I would need to apply for base family housing or get an apartment off base. The fact that my family was staying in South Carolina eliminated the possibility of base housing, so I began looking for an apartment. I was able to stay in a temporary room on base while I was searching. That made life a bit easier. I got introduced to my team, got set up in my new office, settled into my new temporary living quarters, and set up my bank account at the credit union on base. Then, it was time to gamble.

I started buying scratch-off tickets almost immediately. At this point, I chose not to deny or try to fight my obsession. I will say it did start off slowly at first this time. I had a lot of new things to adjust to in my new environment, so I would only gamble periodically. But within a few weeks, the fever returned. During this time, I found an apartment and my first wife sent extra money so I could furnish it, which I did. The apartment was in a less than ideal neighborhood, but the rent was cheap, which left me with more gambling money. I moved myself and all of my new furniture in. I missed my children terribly, but I was happy to be on my own. I was my own boss and didn't answer to anyone. I took full advantage and dove right in.

My life was getting darker by the day. I showed up to work. I did my job…at first, but I was more going through the motions than anything. I could not wait to get through my day and week so I could gamble. I had zero interest in any sort of social activities. My calls home were becoming less. I was able to gamble off my pay and winnings for a while, but eventually, that would run out. I began to sell all of the furniture that I had purchased for the apartment. I found one small loan company and borrowed about $2,000. But because I hadn't paid my debt from South Carolina, my credit score was plummeting, and fewer places were willing to loan me money. I had to get more and more creative to feed my addiction. At one point, I went to an electronics store, applied for in-store credit, which I was approved for, bought a $1,000 laptop computer, took it out of the box, turned in on then off, and took it to a pawnshop and got about 200 bucks for it. I was flat-out desperate! To save rent money, I convinced my command I had a hardship because I was separated from my family, and they allowed me to temporarily move back into the quarters I was in when I first arrived.

At this point, I was out of control. I bounced several checks at the bank on base. This is a huge no-no because, had they reported it to my command, I could have gotten into serious trouble. I was able to keep them from doing that by giving them a complete bullshit story and periodic payments. I was spending everything I had and was not keeping money for food. Because I was in food inspection, and an NCOIC, I was able to go around to units on base and get them to give me cases of MREs (meals) they had in stock. I truthfully don't know exactly how I pulled this off, but I did. I would keep most of these so I could eat, but I would also take some to the military surplus store off base. They were happy to pay about fifty bucks a case since they could sell them for more. I was never caught doing this. Looking back, I wish I had been. Eventually, I did something and did get caught.

I was at a point of absolute desperation in my addiction. I thought about it almost constantly. I could barely focus on work, although I was somehow muddling through. So on a quiet weekend, I walked into my unit, took our digital camera, which was US government property, and took it to the pawnshop. I did it again. I stole from my own unit to feed my gambling addiction. Once again, it didn't take long for the unit to discover the missing camera. Once again, a criminal investigation was started, and once again, I turned myself in. The interview didn't take long. I already had a history of unbecoming actions. I was turned back over to my unit and told to go to my room to await next steps. I went back to my room, again took a handful of painkillers, and began to run, headfirst into the brick wall of my room. I wanted to break my neck. I wanted to fall asleep and not wake up. I wanted anything but to face who I had become. But I was not able to break my own neck. I took myself to the naval hospital and confessed to what I had just done and to my desire to end my own life. I was in a fog at the naval hospital. They did a physical check on me, took my shoelaces and anything else I could hurt myself with, and put me in a room with a guard until the next step, which was to send me to a civilian acute psych facility off base. That happened later that day.

Two Weeks

It was day one of the two weeks I was going to spend at the psych facility. I had just arrived and was being admitted. I was handed a phone. It was my wife asking me what had happened and if I was okay. I was in such a fog I replied incoherently, which I'm sure didn't make things better. The call didn't last long. They finished admitting me and put me in my room, and out I went for the night. I woke up the next morning more rested than I had felt in a long time. Apparently, I was given a sleep aid the day before. I was introduced to my fellow residents and my first inpatient treatment began. I attended groups and made friends with other residents. It was kind of nice to be away from gambling and chaos and stress.

About a week into my stay, my detachment officer and my district commander came for a visit. We sat down in the conference room of the treatment center. I knew this was not a friendly check-in, so I put the wrinkled uniform I came in with on. Sure enough, this meeting was to administer punishment and to tell me I was being put out of the Army. My commander spoke very frankly but also very kindly to me. I remember him telling me how confused he was because he thought I was a good NCO. He told me I would be discharged general under honorable conditions. This was very generous. What I had done could easily have gotten me a dishonorable discharge. He told me the discharge he gave me would allow me to seek the help I needed at the VA once I was out. The problem I had is that no one could tell me what that help was. It was very neat and clean. I had suffered several years of a devastating gambling addiction, yet what I got from the Army was a generous discharge for theft. Don't misunderstand me, I'm grateful for the release I got from the Army, I just wish they had done more to try to understand and treat what I was going through. The Army had and still has a program for soldiers who struggle with alcohol or drugs, but they didn't even make an effort to try to help me. I'm not saying I would have been reformed and went on to have a long career. I'm simply saying it would have been nice to have the chance.

I finished my time at the treatment center and went back to base to begin the process of getting out of the Army. I clearly remember the day I went back to my unit. I sat in a chair in the waiting area, and no one would talk to me or even look at me. I was okay with that because I was so ashamed and embarrassed at that point I just wanted to get out and move on. I out processed the naval air station and then was sent to Fort Sam Houston in San Antonio to finish leaving the Army. That went better for me because I didn't have to see much of my unit there. It took about a day or so. I turned in my military ID card, was escorted to the door of the out-processing center, and was basically told not to let the door hit me in the ass. I drove off post for the last time, drove to the closest military surplus store, sold all of my uniforms and anything I could get a dime for, and I was a civilian.

The Gambling Veteran

Texas

I left the Army in July of 2005, just three and a half years after that night in Korea when I found the slot room that started it all for me. Fortunately, I left the Army under honorable conditions although I would not come to realize the value of that for some time. I also left the Army broke and separated. When I drove off Ft. Sam Houston in 2005, I really didn't have a plan. I was living with one of the patients I had spent two weeks with at the inpatient mental health center. We had become friends, and I would spend weekends at his place while I was awaiting my fate. He had a very cool little house on stilts that sat over an inlet off of Corpus Christi Bay. It was a quiet neighborhood with friendly neighbors. It also offered me an opportunity to fish whenever I wanted. Since my stay at the mental health center, I had discovered fishing. I fished from docks and shores, mostly for red drum, but for whatever I could catch. The biggest thing was that, when I was fishing, I didn't think about gambling.

I left San Antonio and headed back to Corpus Christi, now as a civilian. I needed a job and had heard about a place that collected lab samples from local health-care facilities and transported them to the lab in San Antonio. It was a daily route. The pay wasn't fabulous, but it was pay. So I applied and pretty quickly got the job. For the next few weeks, I worked, fished, and drank nightly with my hosts and new roommates. They were good people but drank quite a bit. I would join them but would often excuse myself. It was a pretty good life for a short time, but I knew this was not where I ultimately wanted to be. I also noticed that I was starting to again stop and pick up lottery tickets while I was at the bait store or mini market picking up beer for my hosts. Slowly, the addiction was creeping in again. About a month or so after leaving the Army and moving in with my friends, I made the decision to go home. I was headed to Pennsylvania.

Pennsylvania

Once I made the decision to go to Pennsylvania, I let my first wife know. She suggested I stop in South Carolina to see the kids, and so we could talk. I thought this was a good idea and agreed. So in August of 2005, I began my journey north. I guess you could say I got lucky on that journey because not long after I drove east on Interstate 10, through Louisiana, hurricane Katrina hit. I was well past there by then but remember feeling a sense of relief that I had made it through. On my journey north and east, I began experiencing trouble with my car. It would move along fine then suddenly just die out along the side of the road. If I let it sit for a bit, it would start, and I could go for a bunch more miles. I called my aunt, who lived in Georgia and was along the way. I asked her if I could stay the night and she didn't hesitate. So I had somewhere to rest later that day.

Between Louisiana and Georgia was Alabama and the small casino I had stopped at on my way to Texas over a year before. I decided to stop to "win some travel cash." I had a couple hundred bucks on me from my last paycheck, so I could easily add to that. I hit the casino. I was excited and couldn't wait to get to the machines. If someone was looking from the outside, I probably would have looked like a puppy whose owner was away for a few days and just got back. I couldn't wait! Well, a couple of hours later, I left that casino flat broke, and unfortunately, I had not gassed up the car before going in. I just knew I was walking out with lots of money, so why bother? I looked at the gas gauge and knew I didn't have enough left to make it to my aunt's place. So I pulled over at a very busy gas station, dug out all of my CDs and DVDs, and had a roadside sale. I was walking around peddling my entertainment like I was trying to make a buck on a New York subway. It took about an hour or so, but I finally sold enough for a half tank of gas and a pack of smokes, and I was off again.

I limped into my aunt's place later that day, car wheezing, me stressed and tired, and ready for a meal and some sleep. I knew I wouldn't make it very far on the couple bucks I had left, but that was a tomorrow problem. My aunt took me in, hugged me, fed me, and gave me a place to sleep. It felt good to just stop for a bit. I had worn myself out. The next morning, I got up and my cousin was there dropping off his daughters. We had worked and lived together years before, and I felt like I had a good relationship with him. I pulled him aside and asked if I could borrow some money because I was having car trouble and needed to get to South Carolina to get it checked. There was some truth in that, but by then I had become skilled at weaving truth into my lies to make them feel more believable. He quickly opened his wallet and gave me a couple hundred bucks. I told him I would pay him back once I was settled in Pennsylvania. In my mind, I had intended to pay him back but also knew it wasn't likely to happen.

I hugged my aunt, hopped in the car, and was on my way to South Carolina. I had the same issue after leaving Georgia. The car would stop periodically. I would let it rest and be on my way. I made it to South Carolina late on the day I left. I pulled into the driveway of a house I had never been to. My first wife had to find a new place to live and found a small house in a development. I was excited to see my children, and they were excited to see me. I took everything out of my car and stored it along the side of her house so I could make room for the kids in the car. I was going to take them out to play later that day. My wife set up an appointment for me the next day to get the car looked at. We were cordial and friendly at that point, but it appeared clear to both of us that getting back together was not an option.

I took the kids out that day. We had a lot of fun. I brought them back and we all had dinner together. That felt good. After putting the children to bed, my first wife and I sat on the front porch. We had a pretty open conversation about what had happened and what life would look like moving forward. We both agreed trying to reconcile was probably not the path to take. It was a good conversation, and I'm glad we had it. The next morning, I took the car to the shop. It didn't take them long to find and fix the problem. I thanked my first wife for a good conversation, hugged the holy crap out of my children, and I was on my way to Pennsylvania.

I had already arranged to stay with my mother until I could get a job and find a place to stay. My wife had given me some travel money, but of course, I gambled it away on the way home. I got to my mother's with no money, very little gas, no job, and a big helping of depression because I had just left my children again. I was happy to be there and quite sad at the same time. My mother always looked out for me. More honestly put, my mother was an enabler. She wanted to see her son happy and would do whatever she could to do that, even if it meant supporting bad habits. I knew I'd have money when I got to Mom's because Mom always came through. So I got some gas in the car and started my job search.

It didn't take long for me to find my first job. Within two weeks of putting out résumés, I had an offer to work as a concrete inspector at a plant not too far from me. I took it because it was close to home and the pay was decent. The job turned out to be pretty rough. The day started as early as 3:30 in the morning and could run until the sun went down. We often worked six days a week. I liked this because I was making pretty good money but hated it because it interfered with my gambling time. When I got back to Pennsylvania, I found a casino not too far away in neighboring Delaware. It was about a forty-five-minute drive from me. So when I got paid, it was the first place I wanted to go. The first time I went, I can remember my heart racing as I was getting closer. I couldn't wait to be back in a casino despite all of the damage I had done. And so the dive into the darkest part of my addiction began.

Jobs, Jobs, and More Jobs

Not very long into my new job, I came to the decision that it was interfering with my gambling time. The job was dirty. There was almost constant concrete dust, and the coloring they would use for the concrete would get on everything. I would go through a pair of boots every six weeks or so because of the acidity of the concrete, and the state inspector was almost constantly on my back. I was okay with all of that. I didn't mind labor. I could tolerate dust. I had dealt with nagging inspectors before. But the hours, and my inability to gamble when I wanted, drove me to find another job. After a few weeks of applying and interviewing, I took a job in a management training program with a fast-food franchise group. It would mean different shifts each week, but I got two days off per week and would again be making decent money.

Things were fairly quiet the first few months on the new job. I gambled, but not all the time. I was quite busy adjusting to the job, which I enjoyed. I liked the challenge of managing schedules, interviewing, and developing employees. But as it seemed to always happen since 2001, eventually the job became routine, and I began to gamble more frequently. I spoke to my children once or twice a week, but I missed them terribly. I still carried all of the weight of what I had done over the last few years, and I was not dealing with it. The casino, now basically an "old friend," offered the escape I wanted and felt like I needed. So my trips to Delaware increased. As usual, as my need to gamble increased, my income did not. I found myself borrowing from my mother until I got paid. I started making excuses as to why I wasn't sending money for my kids. I was even late to work a couple of times although I was very careful not to let that happen too often.

It was only about seven or eight months into my new job, I was working the closing shift. Part of my job at the end of my shift was to count the money taken in that day, put the appropriate amount in the time lock safe for the next day, and take the rest a block down the road to the bank where I would put the deposit through the night deposit window. It was a Saturday night. I knew the bank was closed until Monday, and I was at a point of desperation. The addiction had once again taken over fully. I sat shaking in the manager's office, knowing what I was about to do, and trying feverishly to talk myself out of it. Dr. Jekyll and Mr. Hyde had returned. As dangerous as knew it was, I told myself it would be okay, that I would put it all back, and I took the Friday night deposit bag and drove to Delaware. It was a couple thousand dollars. I had convinced myself I would win enough to put it all back and still have money left over. I did not. I spent it all with the exception of a few dollars I kept for gas and cigarettes.

The next day, I was back at work and acted as if nothing had happened. I was getting really good at hiding my anxiety and fear. I was also getting really good at lying to others and to myself. I spent much of the next day preoccupied and scared. At times I can remember shaking. What had I done? This was not a few bucks from a petty cash fund or a digital camera. This was a couple thousand dollars. This was also the outside world. My military service would have little bearing on what would happen to me if I got caught. I managed to make it through the evening and into the night. I again had to prepare the deposit bag. This time I knew Monday was coming, and the bags would be counted. I felt trapped in a snare of my own making. I got through the night, cleaned up, put the appropriate amount of money in the time lock safe, prepared the deposit bag, and headed to the casino.

As I drove toward the casino early that Monday morning, I was scared to death. I needed to win back all of the money I had taken. I didn't care if there was anything left for me. I just had to replace what I took so I could keep my job and not get in trouble. I was sweating. I was talking to myself the whole way there. I even cried at one point. Yet at the same time there was a sense of excitement. There was a sense of relief that I was going to my "safe place," and I kept telling myself everything was going to be okay. To have these opposing trains of thought happening at the same time was dizzying. I knew I was crazy. I knew there was something terribly wrong with me. My heart broke as a realized what I had done to my employer, and what I was doing to myself and my family, and I felt free. I felt excited. I felt like I was where I needed to be. To try to describe these things to someone who has never experienced them is next to impossible. To be sure, at the time I thought no one could *ever* understand what was happening to me. Yet it made sense, and I drove on.

We had closed early that night, so I think I made it to the casino around midnight or so. I remember walking in, and all of that fear and anxiety melted away. It was my night, and I was going to fix everything. I did not fix everything. In fact, I had used all but about a hundred dollars by about five in the morning. I decided to take what I had left and leave. I was worn out, mentally and physically. I got in the car and started driving back toward Pennsylvania. I had to make a decision. I was either going to turn myself in because I wouldn't hide, or I was going to end it all. This was my entire trip, flipping between the two. If I was going to end it, how would I do it? Where would I do it? Should I leave a note? If I was going to turn myself in, would I go to my employer or straight to the police? I shook the entire time. I was also dead tired and, at the end of the trip, decided I would turn myself in to the police and let my fate be decided from there.

I arrived at the police station in the morning, I guess around 7:00 AM or so. I walked in with the deposit bag and the remaining money I had. I had both deposit slips with me. I went to the front desk and simply said I was turning myself in for theft. I was escorted to an interview room and asked to wait until the detective arrived. It wasn't long until someone walked in and the questions and answers began. I explained who I was and where I worked. I gave him my vice president's number so he could contact her. I answered all of his questions honestly. In that moment, I had given up. I was just plain tired and couldn't take it anymore. We finished the interview, he let me grab a cigarette, then put me in a holding cell until he knew what was happening next. My boss, the vice president of the franchise group, showed up a short time later. She wasn't angry. She said she was confused to which my response was "so am I." I didn't understand what was happening to me other than the fact that the need to gamble had been all-consuming, and I obviously would do about anything to feed that need. She thanked me for turning myself in and was on her way. Not too much later, I was released and given an initial court date for arraignment.

A week later, I was at my arraignment hearing where it was decided I would be tried. I was told to go to the county courthouse and talk to the bail office because I was now out on bail until my trial, which was to be a few months later. I took care of that the same day. I was, of course, fired from my job. The odd thing is that my boss said she had considered keeping me on, but that I definitely needed help for what was going on with me. I thanked her and told her I would have declined had she offered to keep me. I didn't want the risk of doing what I had just done again.

Shortly after I had gotten back to Pennsylvania, I traded in the car I had for a used Honda. I didn't trust the car I came back with. Now because I had lost my job, and because I had gambled so much, I didn't make payments, the car got repossessed. I was without a car and without a job. Mom to the rescue! Okay, not Mom to the rescue, more like "time to take advantage of Mom." She had a car she rarely used since she retired, so I offered to "keep it running" for her. I also borrowed (took) some money from her until I could find a new job. She was happy to help, not knowing I was using some of the money to gamble. I didn't have enough for casino trips, so I went back to scratch-off lottery for a while.

It again didn't take long for me to find another job. A local restaurant was looking for a host and manager. I applied and pretty quickly got the job. The position was for a new location that had recently been opened. I started and adjusted pretty quickly. I worked odd hours at first, but eventually got into a consistent schedule. It could get extremely busy, but I enjoyed the pace and enjoyed the paycheck because I was back to gambling. I got paid cash, so it was an easy trip to the casino on payday. By this time my paycheck was often gone not long after I got it, usually within a day or two, sometimes within a few hours. I did win once. I was playing a slot machine and hit the jackpot. It wasn't a huge jackpot. I think it was maybe $1,200 or $1,500, but it refueled me. I stayed and played until I was too tired. I then went to a local hotel and got a room. I slept for a couple of hours and was back in the casino bright and early the next morning. I needed to "strike while the iron was hot" and turn that money into more. Yeah, that didn't work. I spent pretty much the entire next day in the casino and left with nothing. By this point, I beginning to know this would be the outcome every time I went to the casino, but Mr. Hyde wasn't having that. The addicted part of me just knew I was going to win big, pay everything off, and quit forever even though reality told a much different story.

I was back to work. We were short on servers, and someone was sent from another restaurant. She arrived, and I was immediately smitten. She was a bright, overly friendly, smart, witty woman with a ton of energy, and I needed to know her because she was everything I couldn't be at that point in my life. We became friends pretty quickly although I felt like I wanted more. She stayed working at the restaurant I was managing, and after a while, she invited me to hang out at her place. I accepted like a kid on Christmas morning. It turned out she lived with her mother and brother. It also turned out she struggled with a drug addiction. But my ego was being fed and I felt good. So in addition to gambling whenever I could, I was now also taking this woman to different places to help her get drugs and feed her addiction. I felt like I was helping her, like we were a team. What I was really doing was enabling and being a driver.

During this time, I went for my trial for the money I had stolen from my prior employer. Because it was a first-time offense, and because I was a military veteran, they put me on a program that allowed me to pay restitution and attend regular meetings with a probation officer. If I did this over a period of time, and paid off my restitution, my record would be expunged. This was yet another opportunity to walk away clean, and I took it happily. I was back at work, and the owners, who were showing increased confidence in me, were also giving me increased responsibility, including (you guessed it) counting the money and preparing the deposit at the end of the night. And after a while (you guessed it), I took money and gambled with it. This time I was able to win enough to put the money back. I can't begin to describe the level of fear I experienced when I was gambling with this money. But that did not stop the compulsion to do it. Thankfully, I had enough sense to put that money back.

I was looking over my shoulder daily at work, wondering if anyone had noticed what I had done. No one did, but I worked in fear every day. I was also noticing my friendship with the server who seemed to need me more for access to drugs than anything was getting tiresome. Please don't get me wrong. Beneath what she was dealing with was a remarkable human being. But like me, her addiction was in control. And if I'm being honest, helping her feed her addiction was interfering with my ability to feed mine. I decided to quit that job and find another.

While I was working at the restaurant, I moved out of my mother's place and rented a room. This room was in a house owned by a gentleman who was only there every now and then. I basically had the run of the house, although I spent most of my time in my room. I was now making regular trips to the casino and buying scratch-off lottery to fill in the time between casino trips. I was gambling whenever I could. I was almost always out of money and leaving my job at the restaurant didn't help. I was experiencing severe bouts of depression. I can remember lying in bed with the shades down, the lights off, and the TV on for days at a time because I had again gambled myself into nothing. I bounced a rent check to my landlord. He knew something was not right with me. My mother helped me cover the check, but he very kindly asked me to move out. He had a young son and didn't want anything stressing that relationship. My addiction had once again done damage to a relationship with a good person. So I moved back to Mom's. As I was cleaning out the room, I went to take out the bed. It was a single bed. As I went to remove the mattress, the entire frame lifted slightly. I looked and couldn't believe what I saw. I had stuffed so many scratched lottery tickets under that bed that it had lifted the frame off the floor. If I had to guess, I would say there was close to $10,000 in scratch-off tickets in that pile. I knew I needed help. Still, how could anyone possibly understand?

While I was living in that house, a few other things happened. My divorce with my first wife was finalized, and she told me she had started seeing someone. I was happy for her but wondered what would happen with my children. I also traded in my mother's car for a jeep Wrangler so I could drive in the snow. That Wrangler, which had over a hundred thousand miles on it, died not long after I bought it. My brother agreed to give me a car he was going to get rid of anyway. It was small and had a broken mirror, but it was free. I had also started going to the VA. I wanted to see someone to see if I could figure out what was going on with me and how I could fix it because doing it on my own wasn't working.

The Trip

It was a Friday, right after I had left the restaurant, and was moving out of my room and back to my mother's. I had the car my brother had given to me and a couple hundred bucks I had borrowed because my last paycheck from the job I had just left wouldn't be in for a couple of days. I had no job and nothing to do. I was depressed and felt hopeless. Naturally, a trip to the casino was in order. It felt like the only thing that brought me any comfort at that point. My meetings with counselors at the VA seemed useless to me. One therapist drew relationship circles and talked to me about the importance of good relationships. A psychiatrist sat and talked to me for ten minutes then told me I was bipolar and gave me a prescription. I laughed at her and left. Nothing felt like it was working, and off to my old friend, my safe place I went. I was driving toward the casino. By now, another casino had opened near me. It was still almost an hour away but in the same state and something newer than the one in Delaware. I was on the road. Dr. Jekyll and Mr. Hyde were in full battle mode.

I can remember driving down the road and punching the roof of the car, literally yelling at myself to turn around because I knew I would walk out of that casino broke, depressed, ashamed, and afraid. Then Mr. Hyde would chime in "This is the time! This is the one! My problems are solved today! It feels good…" I remember looking in the mirror at one point. My face was bright red and there were tears on my cheeks. Yet my foot stayed on the gas pedal, and I continued toward the casino. I pulled into the parking garage of the casino. I was still angry, afraid, and filled with anxiety. I still walked to the door. I opened it and stepped in. I heard the sounds of machines spinning and people chattering, and I smelled the smells and felt the atmosphere. In that moment, every bit of fear, anxiety, worry, anger, and everything else I wasn't willing to deal with went away. It simply went away like someone had just shot me with a giant helping of happy juice. I was fully down the rabbit hole.

I walked in the casino that Friday and found my machine. I was happy. At least for a while the world was outside of the door that I had just walked in. I felt free, and I began to play. I played through the day, winning enough to keep myself going. I hit small jackpots a few times. I walked in there with about five hundred bucks and, at one point, was up about three grand or so. I continued to play. If I could make three grand, why not five or ten? I drank the drinks they would bring me, mixing in an occasional water or coffee. I did not eat. I didn't have time. At times, I would have to go to the bathroom so badly I thought I was going to go right there but was unwilling to leave the machine. Fortunately, I made it to the bathroom each time, but I slowed down my drinking knowing it would lead to the need for a bathroom break. I was up. I was down then I was up again. But eventually, down started happening more than up, and eventually, as had always happened, I ran out of money.

By this time, I had reached a point where I couldn't wait to lose the money that I had left but refused to get up and leave until it was gone. Let me say that again. I couldn't wait to lose the small amount of money I had left, yet I refused to get up and leave until all of my money was gone. What an insane and abusive addiction! I did finally run out of money and knew it was time to go. I figured I was there overnight and that was long enough. I walked out to the car and started it. When the radio came on, there was a religious show on. I was surprised to hear a religious show on a Saturday morning until I turned the station and discovered it was Sunday. I had not been in that casino overnight. I had been in there for a day and a half! I didn't eat for a day and a half and didn't notice it. I was up for thirty-six hours straight and didn't notice it. I was sick and I knew it. But it didn't end there.

I drove home as depressed, if not more depressed, than I had ever been. I had just spent thirty-six hours in a casino without a second thought. My children were ten hours away, and I barely spoke with them. I had no job because I had either quit or been fired from three jobs in about a year and a half. I was a fully grown adult living with my mother. I carried the weight of everything that had happened since Korea, and I didn't know how nor did I want to deal with any of it. I spent part of the rest of that day sleeping. It was restless sleep, but my body wasn't going any longer without it. That evening, I drove to the local grocery store parking lot. Parking lots seemed to be my safe spaces. I could think there without being interrupted. Okay, I could hide there without being interrupted.

I can remember sitting in a parking lot a few weeks before talking with my brother. He was tough on me but was the one person who I felt didn't judge what I was feeling. He was simply there for me. I never listened though. So I was in the grocery store parking lot for a few hours when I decided to just take a bunch of the antidepressant pills I had with me. Maybe I could fall asleep and not wake up. Maybe if I took them all of this shame and guilt and confusion over what was happening to me would just go away. But not long after I took them, I got scared. I again don't think I really wanted to end my life. I wanted to end my misery. I wanted this to stop. I wanted someone to tell me how to fix this shit show I was living in. I took myself to the local hospital where I was given a hefty helping of charcoal slurry to counteract the antidepressants. I was later told that much antidepressant could cause severe seizures. I was put on watch overnight.

The next morning, the doctor checked in on me, and I was feeling much better. He took me off suicide watch, and they wanted to put me in a psychiatric ward for a few days. Here's the thing. That morning, I realized that my last paycheck from the restaurant was probably sitting in my mailbox. I kindly turned the doctor down. They proceeded to tell me that if I was going to leave the hospital, I would need to sign a form stating that I was leaving against medical advice. Naturally, I did. I left the hospital dizzy, tired, and (please pardon the gross) peeing black from the charcoal. That didn't matter. I drove home, got the check from mailbox, took it to the local Walmart and cashed it, and was on my way back to the casino the next day. I gambled away that check in a few hours. I was spinning, depressed, ashamed, and angry. Here we go again! I drove myself to the VA hospital and checked in because I was once again in a mood to hurt myself. This time I was there for a week.

I left the VA hospital after about a week of medication, group therapy, and individual therapy. We talked about depression and family and coping skills, but I can't remember one session or conversation where we talked about gambling. I left the hospital feeling a bit more grounded, but hardly "cured." I went back to my mother's to find out that my ex-wife and children were there for a visit. I put on my best face and hugged the shit out of my kids. My ex and I spoke briefly. She asked if I was okay. I said yeah. I said I thought the week in the VA had done me a lot of good, and I needed the break. I was lying. While I did feel a bit more grounded, I was still lost and had no idea where to turn for help. The visit with the children was good. They all left later that day. That would be the last time I would see them for almost three years.

Rock Bottom

Not too many days after I got out of the VA hospital, I was back to gambling. I had taken day work from a "work today, get paid today" place right down the road from my mother's. They would have me do things like construction cleanup or dropping flyers on houses and would pay me daily. It became a viscous cycle…work, pay, spend, broke, work, pay, spend, broke. I was going to weekly counselor visits at the VA but felt I was getting nowhere. I didn't eat anymore except when I absolutely had to, and then it was mostly bagged snacks and other junk. I was smoking almost three packs of cigarettes a day, most of which I got from my mother. I was a shell. I didn't interact with anyone. I didn't want to interact with anyone. I felt completely empty. Even gambling wasn't filling the void anymore. I just gambled because I did. I went to bed every night praying I wouldn't wake up but was too afraid to do anything about it because I would likely just end up screwing it up and ending up in the psych ward again.

I had reached my first rock bottom. This is a term talked about often in addiction treatment and in twelve-step programs like alcoholics or Gamblers Anonymous, but until I had experienced it for myself, you would have had a really hard time trying to describe it to me. It was a feeling of complete despair, of complete hopelessness, and that there would never be a way out no matter what I did. I had given up. I was tired of fighting. I had looked online for treatment centers that deal with gamblers but couldn't find any. I didn't want just any treatment. I wanted something that could tell me why the hell I gambled so damn much and what I needed to do to get past it. Then I went to a counseling session at the VA. I was seeing a new counselor that day. After speaking with me a while, she pulled out a packet of papers. She said it was for a VA-run gambling treatment program outside of Cleveland, Ohio. She told me I would have to do the work and handed me the packet. I was skeptical, but I was also so lost at that point I had nothing to lose, so I called the number on the packet, and I would be introduced to a whole new world.

Introduction to Recovery Introduction to Relapse

Recovery...Or So I Thought

It was June of 2007. It was just under two years since I had been put out of the Army for very unbecoming conduct due to a gambling addiction. In that short time, I managed to go through four jobs, rob an employer, sell my mother's car and go through two others, steal from another employer and put it back, and gamble myself to the edge of oblivion. I hated myself and everything I had become. I was unwilling to face the shit that made me this way. I tried to tough out the addiction. I tried to outthink the addiction. I tried everything I knew how to do. Nothing worked! So now I was going to give the VA in Brecksville, Ohio, a shot.

I drove to Cleveland in the car my brother gave me. I purposely did not take the Pennsylvania Turnpike, which would have been the fastest way there, because I had already planned on a "last hoorah" on the way there. I was going to gamble one more time. I came to find out later this is not unusual. Gambling had become part of my daily existence despite my hatred for what it had done to me. It was familiar and a safe haven for me, and I was going to do it one more time before I gave it up completely. Yep, I was convinced I was about to put gambling behind me forever.

I stopped and gambled overnight at a casino along the way. I found it boring, but necessary. I gambled until the sun was coming up then got in the car and finished my trip to Brecksville. I didn't know what to expect when I got there, so I stopped for a fast-food breakfast and a cup of coffee in case I was going on lockdown. I was ready for anything because I had literally given up. I wanted help and knew I wasn't going to get it on my own. I got to the VA hospital. They took me in and gave me a brief physical check. I was stunned. I am six feet one inch and normally weighed somewhere between 190 and 200 pounds. I weighed in at 165 pounds. I hadn't weighed that little since somewhere around eighth grade. After seeing that weight, I went into the bathroom and pulled up my shirt. I could see my ribs. I also noticed how pale and drawn I looked. I was literally strung out without any help from any sort of drug or other substance. I was a shell, mentally and physically. I got processed in and was taken to the wing where I would be given a room. It had a locked door, so I was sure this would be a lockdown ward. But I didn't care. As it turns out, it wasn't. I was shown to my room, given a urine test, then told where the smoking area was outside and that I had to be in the area by a certain time because the doors would be closed and locked. Okay, some freedom anyway.

Within my first week being in the program, I received a certified letter. It was from the county in South Carolina where my ex-wife and children were living. The letter stated that a court hearing had been held, and it was decided that I was to be stripped of parental rights. When I got this letter, I had reached just about my lowest point and was in no position to fight this or deal with it. So in that moment, I let it go. The next day I went to my first group and was introduced to my fellow veterans struggling with gambling. All of their gambling was different. One was hooked on poker, another on slot machines like me, still another was hooked on a form of video gambling that was the only thing available where she was from. But all of us had something in common. We were all completely hooked on gambling and didn't know how to stop. That first day, also in that first group, I also met my therapist. She was a small woman with a tiny voice. She started talking to us and asked us what we wanted from our time there. When she got to me, I said, "I just want to do it right." She immediately responded with "Fuck right! Just be honest." I found out right then and there that small woman with the tiny voice would be a force to be reckoned with. I later discovered she was, and still is, a very well-known worldwide authority on gambling addiction and treatment. But in that moment, I knew I was in the right place.

I got to know my therapist and my teammates better. I also got to know the other therapists that were there. Knowing these amazing people has helped me more times than I can say, which you'll see as you read on. We got deeper into understanding gambling as an addiction. I would talk to veterans who were there for other addictions while I was on breaks or at the end of the day. I discovered that what we were going through, and some of the things we had done weren't all that different. It seemed that addiction was about more than the drug or drink or slot machine. There was something deeper. One of our assignments was to write an autobiography. We needed to be honest about ourselves and our journey through addiction. I wrote mine and turned it in. She gave it back to me and said try again. "What? Why?" was my response. She told me it wasn't honest. Maybe the stories were accurate, but I needed more. I needed to be truly honest about how it felt. So back at it I went. I dug deep. I filled twelve legal-sized pages with that autobiography. More importantly, for the first time probably ever, I began to open the vault that I had created for myself. She read the revised copy and simply said, "Better." Then the shocker came. We each had to sit in front of our fellow veterans and read our autobiographies. It was bad enough I had to write this shit, now I have to read it? I have to read it in front of other people?! I did. We all did. There were a lot of tears. I felt a lot of fear. When it was over, I was shaking, but I felt a sense of relief I had never felt. Thank goodness that was on a Friday because I slept like a baby until noon the next day. I was wiped.

We were told that while we were in this program, we would need to attend Gamblers Anonymous. Cleveland had a very active GA community, and there was a meeting right at the VA each week so that's where I attended my first meeting. I had heard of twelve-step programs before, where people say "Hi, I'm so and so and I'm an alcoholic," and everyone shouts "Hi" and sings "Kum ba yah." Yep, I was skeptical. I had thoughts of cult running through my head walking into that first meeting, but it was part of our program, so I went. I sat down and they read out of a yellow book. Today I know very well what that book says, but back then, it might as well have been Charlie Brown's teacher squawking like a trombone with a mute in it. Oh well, at least there was free coffee and snacks. They got through the reading, and someone got up to start talking about his gambling addiction and the damage it had done.

As I listened, something happened. I felt like he was telling my story! Sure, the circumstances and people and places were different, but it was me. How the hell did he know about me? He finished, everyone clapped, and the next person got up. Wait a minute! She knows my story too! What's going on here? I began to see a pattern. People would get up and talk, and each one of them would say something I could identify with. I was beginning to understand that not only was I not alone as a gambling veteran, but I was not alone as someone who struggles with a gambling addiction, period. And while all of our stories were different, we were not unique. We had a similar cause and similar feelings. I got my first exposure to the understanding of the power of connection. It would be many more years until I truly began to understand that, but at least I had been given a glimpse.

Be Happy, with Crappy

I wrote a book called be *Happy with Crappy*. A lot of people that saw this title thought that this meant that we should just be happy, even when life is sucking. While I aspire to this, it's not where this title came from. I spent the better part of my life hiding from my feelings. I learned early on that expressing my feelings usually led to painful consequences, and the Army taught me, from day one that mission comes first and there really isn't a place for feelings on the battlefield. So I hid my feelings. In fact, I'd probably go as far as to say I really didn't know how to feel my feelings. Sure, I could show sadness or worry, but I wasn't really capable of feeling them because I didn't know how. One of the things the program at the VA was teaching me was how to tap into these feelings so I could experience them, and then allow them to go on their way. Mindfulness was a big part of the reason I was able to learn this. In mindfulness, I learned how to get in touch with where I was in any given moment and just sit with what came up, whether it was thoughts or feelings. I was hardly an expert, but I was beginning to better understand that feelings were not the eight-hundred-pound bear I had always made them out to be. So I was starting to allow myself to feel.

One day I was in a one-on-one session with my therapist. We talked briefly about group and about things going on that day. Then she asked me how I was feeling. I told her I wasn't sure, and of course, she asked why. I said I was feeling very happy overall. I felt good, and I felt like my recovery was going well. But I was also struggling with a personal issue that made me sad. I don't remember exactly what the issue was, other than I believe it was something going on with one of my fellow veterans. So I said I wasn't sure which to feel, happy or sad. She said, "Why not both?" This took place many years ago, so I don't remember all of the details of what happened, but I very clearly remember the confusion I felt when she asked me that question. I said, "What?" She again said, "Why not both?" I told her you can't do that. She asked why not. I told her you couldn't feel two feelings, especially two opposite feelings at the same time. She said, "Yes, you can." I said, "You can? You mean you can feel happy and crappy at the same time?" A simple "yep" was all I got.

And in that moment, a light came on. It was one of those aha moments where I realized I didn't know what I didn't know. My therapist was full of great exercises like this. Some of them admittedly felt a little weird. Once she had me stare at a chair and convince myself I didn't know what it was. By this time, I knew that everything she did had a purpose, so I didn't question it. I just did it. Naturally, within a few minutes, I was questioning the true nature of this object in front of me. I knew it was a chair, but I had become curious about its journey and what trees was it made from and who had sat in it. It opened me up toward a new way of thinking and, more importantly, acceptance.

The four weeks I spent in that inpatient program seemed to fly by. We reached the end, and it was time to say goodbye to my new friends. But I was not going anywhere. I had decided to stay and move into the domiciliary. This was essentially a barracks-style homeless shelter for veterans that just happened to be on VA property. I moved into a room with three other veterans but had my own space. We had to be in by 9:00 PM each night but were free to roam around campus during the day and could go into town as long as we signed out and were back on time. I enrolled in the gambling aftercare program with my therapist and enrolled in an additional trauma therapy group. I also regularly attended multiple Gamblers Anonymous groups in the area. I had made quite a few friends there and had become very comfortable sharing and felt I got a lot from it. At this point, I was only thirty days separated from my addiction, but I was beginning to feel stronger and more like who I wanted to be.

For anyone reading this who might be struggling with a gambling addiction or early in recovery, this is a point in recovery to pay close attention. We can often go through something known as the pink cloud. This is an almost euphoric period of time early in recovery. And it's what I was going through at this time although I didn't know it. We've put enough time and space between our addiction and that now feels really good. It just feels like everything's right in the world and it's all going to be okay. For someone new to recovery, this can be dangerous because we can start to let go of the things that got us to this point. I won't say I did that at this point, but I will say it planted the seed for trouble I would experience later. But in that moment, life felt good. I was going to groups and GA. I had a small job too. I was enrolled in what the VA calls incentive therapy or IT. I was given a job to sweep and mop the second floor of the domiciliary daily. For this, I was paid a small stipend. So I could by smokes, put gas in my car, and enjoy the occasional trip to the coffee shop in town. It was balanced for me. I felt like I was really starting to get this recovery thing.

My car eventually started giving me trouble, so I sold it to a fellow patient. I was up front about the issues and didn't get much for it. I had plenty of new friends with cars and I was learning the bus lines, so I was okay. My therapy was going well too. We were digging deeper. My trauma therapist had me sit and do an exercise in which I was to go back to a time when something traumatic happened to me. When I did, I could literally smell the smells and feel the air on my face from that event. It scared me because all of the traumatic feelings came up too. He told me to sit with them. I really didn't want to and made sure he knew that. He said he knew, but to do it anyway, so I did. It was painful, to be sure. But eventually, the feelings began to subside and eventually they went away. But it was quite a different feeling because they went away on their own. I didn't try to push them away. This was another exercise I wouldn't come to truly begin to appreciate until much later.

On the Town

My next move was to a transitional residence, and my next level of work therapy. The transitional house, or TR, was a house in town. It had several apartments. Each had three or four bedrooms with a common living room and kitchen area. I moved in and met my roommates. They were good guys and, of course, veterans. I also enrolled in compensated work therapy or CWT. This was more structured work with higher pay. My job was to take patients at the main VA hospital, in Cleveland, to their physical therapy appointments in wheelchairs. I took the bus to and from the hospital every day. I had to sign out when I left and sign back in when I returned, and we were subject to periodic urine screenings. I fell into this routine pretty quickly and enjoyed the work I was doing at the hospital. When I was home in my apartment, I would work on my paperwork to try to claim service-connected disability from the VA. Between that, the TV, and puzzles we had, I kept busy. I was to be at the TR for six months. About three months in, I got a regular job. I was allowed to do this as long as I met curfew and maintained a bank account. The job was sales and I fell into it quickly. It was fast-paced and exciting, and I started meeting daily goals pretty quickly. But there was a challenge. About a month into my job, we were supposed to take a few days to go to Columbus, which was a couple of hours away. It would involve overnight stays. By now, I had bought a used car, so I had a way to get back and forth, but the trip was too far to work every day. So I talked with the house manager. He said if I was going away for more than a night, I would need to move out of the house. So I took all of my possessions, put them in the car, and off to Columbus I went.

Lapse

I needed somewhere to live when I got back from Columbus. Fortunately, a friend I had been in my aftercare with, and who I hung out at the coffee shop with, had rented a house in Cleveland Heights, not far from the VA hospital. He had a room and said I could rent it. Unfortunately, right after I got back from Columbus, my car died and I decided to leave the job I left the TR for. Just trying to get to work was getting too stressful and the hours were getting more intense. But before the car died, I lapsed. In Gamblers Anonymous, and in treatment, we talk about relapse. It's a fall from the things were doing to stay in recovery and a return to addictive behaviors. I was not fully there yet. But upon returning from Columbus, and just before moving in with my friend, I took a trip to a casino in Erie, Pennsylvania. It was almost two hours from Cleveland. I don't know what drove me to go there other than the stress of what I was going through at the time. But I went and I spent several hours there. It felt good, but not great. I felt dirty. When I left, I still had money. It was less than I walked in the casino with, but unlike previous experiences at the casino, I was able to walk out before I was fully broke. I never admitted to that, and it feels good to admit to it now.

I moved in with my friend and found another job. This was on the other side of town. It was a telemarketing job selling trash bags and lamps to help support a veterans' organization. I did well at this almost immediately because I am a veteran. It made opening the conversation easier. I worked midday, into the evening, and my trip was long. I had to take a bus to the train station on the east end of town. Take the train completely across town to the west end then either take another bus or walk. It was anywhere from and hour and a half to two hours each way, but I didn't mind it. I had again settled and was not gambling. I was also journaling at night. Journaling was a great way to get my thoughts and feelings out and put them somewhere instead of keeping them bottled up. One night, I started journaling. I can remember the night because it was cold and snowy, a regular day in the winter in Cleveland. I laid down in bed, picked up the notebook and pen, and started to write. An hour or so later, I picked up the pen, not even really knowing what I wrote. I went back and read what I had written. It became a chapter in my first book. I continued to write, using the long train ride to do most of the writing, and penned the first draft of *Be Happy with Crappy: A Journey Through Trauma, Addiction, Rock Bottom, and Recovery* during those rides. It was quite cathartic for me.

I was working and writing every day. I had also enrolled in online school and liked living where I was. What I was not doing was going to Gamblers Anonymous meetings or aftercare, or any kind of recovery activity for that matter. I felt good. I felt like "I got this." Maybe I felt like I was cured. But addiction doesn't work that way. I heard people say recovery was an everyday process and that we needed to take it "a day at a time," but I was good. I didn't need all of that. Sure, I had that trip to the casino, but it was a one-time event, and I was over it. My job was going well, and my life was going well, so why rock the boat, right?

The Girl from Back Home

I was using the laptop I got for school to get on a new fun thing called Facebook. I could connect with friends from all over and see what they were doing. I spoke to friends from high school I hadn't seen for years. I made new friends. I played silly mafia games. I also connected with an old friend of my brother's I had only met once or twice years before. We began to talk and very quickly realized we were feeling something from the conversations. These talks escalated very quickly, and before we knew it, we were using words like *love* and talking about when we were going to see each other. In recovery, they say not to engage in anything too heavy, such as new relationships, for at least a year. There's a good reason for this. That euphoric feeling of someone paying special attention to you can cause a dopamine rush that can rival addiction. During that first year, we're learning to regulate and balance our feelings. A case of the "jitters" can upset that apple cart very quickly. And that's exactly what happened to me. I was "in love" and I knew it. My roommate tried to warn me, but I wasn't having it. I had to see her as soon as possible! So I took a train to Pennsylvania and spent most of my time with her.

The first trip to Pennsylvania was nothing short of nuts. It was a whirlwind of two of us expressing quite a bit in a short period of time. I did visit my mother while I was home but spent most of the time with her then headed back to Cleveland. But it wasn't long before we were planning to see each other again. This time she would drive out to see me. I was still working but had let my schoolwork slide and was not journaling anymore. I simply didn't see the need because life was so good. A few weeks later, she drove out to see me. She stayed for a few days. I took her out to see my work and around the town. When she was ready to go back, I decided I would go back with her then come back to Cleveland. I drove her home. It was one of the most exciting periods of my life and rivaled the height of my gambling addiction. She made my ego feel good! That was all there was to it. But I discovered something on that second trip. She too struggled. She struggled with drugs, specifically prescription pills. She said she was managing fibromyalgia, but she managed it more regularly than the bottle recommended, and she needed more than the doctor would allow. This should have been an immediate red flag for me. It had happened to me before. But I was so smitten at that point it didn't matter. I spent the next week or so with her then it was time to go back. She suggested we drive back together. She and her daughter would go with me then drive back. I thought it was a good idea. We packed up the car and were on our way. We barely made it out of town and got pulled over. It turns out her inspection was overdue. I was driving, so I gave the officer my license. The next thing I know, he's asking me to step out of the car, reading me my rights, and putting on handcuffs. As it turned out, there was a warrant for my arrest. I stopped paying the restitution payments that had been set up for me in 2006, and even though my probation officer knew I was going to Cleveland, I stopped contacting her. I had violated the terms of the probation that could have gotten my record expunged. This was not moving in the right direction.

I was taken to the local jail for processing then moved to the county prison. It was Friday, specifically it was the Friday before Memorial Day, which meant I would not see anyone until the following Tuesday. I was going to be imprisoned for three days, at least, and I was scared to death! I had never been to any kind of jail. At the county prison, I was taken into a room, told to strip down and shower, dried off, had powder thrown all over me, then was given underwear and scrubs that were too big for me. I was given a stack of clothing and bedding then taken into a big common area that was surrounded by two floors of cells with a guard post right in the middle. I was taken to my cell. It was pretty much right out of a movie. It had two very skinny concrete bunkbeds with a thin pad on top. A stainless steel toilet sat pretty much right in the middle of the cell, along the wall. There were no bars, but a door with a small window.

I had a cellmate, but to be honest, I don't remember ever meeting him. I laid down the first night and silently cried until I fell asleep, probably two hours later. I didn't want anyone to hear me because I was fearful of what might happen if they did, so I buried my face in the pillow.

The next morning, we were woken up, brought "online" for accountability, then allowed to take showers before breakfast. The shower was barely wider than me, and I think I felt dirtier after getting out of the shower than I did going in. But shower I did, and then put on new underwear and scrubs that were still too big for me. I went down to the common area to have breakfast. I said nothing to anyone. It's hard to describe how much fear I felt being in that environment, but there was no way I would show it. The food was cold and disgusting, but I ate it because I needed to. We then pretty much just roamed around the common area. At one point, a guard called me out to the guard post. He took me down a hallway and through a door. At the end of a long hallway, he told me I needed to see the counselor, and to walk down the hallway to the end, then turn down another hallway and I would find it. No one walked with me, and as I walked down the hallway, I started to cry uncontrollably. It was so bad it almost dropped me to my knees. I'm not sure what brought it on, but I'm guessing it was the stress, fear, and anxiety of what was happening to me, which was all new. I made it to the counselor, and he allowed me to call my mother, which was comforting. The woman I was seeing was there with her, and I was glad to able to talk to her as well. I felt calmer. The counselor also told me that I would probably see a judge on Tuesday and that I would most likely be let go on bail. That was also a comfort.

Pennsylvania...Again

The following Tuesday I did meet with a judge, and I was set free on bail. I was told a trial date would be set, and I was not to leave the state. My days in Ohio were over. I told my roommate in Cleveland what was happening. He was so angry with me that he would not talk to me and would not send my things to me. I'm not sure what he did with them, but I wasn't too concerned. I let it and my stuff and my roommate and Cleveland go. I was with a woman I thought I loved and back home, and that was enough. At least I thought it was enough. I took a job with a friend of mine doing accounting and organizing for a local shop. It didn't pay a ton, but it was work and I had my small monthly VA check. My friend would pick me up and drop me off, and I would walk everywhere else. I spend a lot of time at my girlfriend's house, but it seemed to get stranger the longer I was there. She became more distant. I also noticed she was using increasing amounts of medications. Despite noticing all of this, I didn't want to let go. I was hooked on the good feeling of having someone who "loved" me. I think I knew better, but I just didn't want to let go.

During this time, something pretty amazing happened. My ex-wife reached out to me. She asked if I would like to talk to my children, who I hadn't spoken with in just over two years. I had a phone call with them, and it went really well. After the call, I cried for nearly a half hour. I had thought about them just about every day over those two years and often wept when I thought about them. Not long after that phone call, they came to Pennsylvania, and I was able to spend a day with my children. They had a lot of questions that day, and I answered them as best I could for two young children. They said they were just happy to have the time with me. It was the beginning of building new relationships with them. I will remember that day as long as I live.

After a few months, I found a job with a manufacturing company through a temp agency. I had to take second shift because it was forty-five minutes away by car, and I needed to take the bus. The bus only ran at certain times and took almost two hours to get where I was going. Still, I was grateful to have the work. My relationship came to an abrupt halt at the same time. She simply stopped answering my calls and texts. I continued to try. She continued to ignore my outreach. I went into a depression, feeling lost and betrayed. I did a bunch of self-help reading. It did help a bit, but what helped the most was my new job. I felt like I was part of a good organization. I started off as a production employee, but eventually worked my way up to a leadership role. During this time, I also had my trial. I was found guilty of theft from three years earlier and put on probation and restitution repayment. This time there would be no missing appointments or payments because if I did, I was sure to do prison time, and after the experience I had that Memorial Day weekend, there was no way in hell I was doing prison time!

I faithfully made it to work every day. I had to ask a good friend for rides home at night because I didn't have a car and the buses didn't run when I was done work. He gave me a ride every night until I was able to get my own car a month or so later. I was also becoming more comfortable being alone and beginning to realize that the relationship I was in was more codependent than anything. While I am grateful for the time I had with her, I also know it never would have lasted and that it was more about each of us trying to fill a void than it was about love. In that time, I had also finished my first book and it hit the market. I was in no position to spend any money promoting it, and this was before the explosion of social media as a marketing tool. So I put a link on Facebook and hoped someone would buy it.

The Room

After some time, I was ready to look for a place to live. I didn't have enough to rent an apartment. I found a room for rent and went to meet the owner. He owned a construction company and had a nice house in the woods that sat back off the road with a stream running right in front. He lived alone and was looking for someone to help offset his costs. The rent was low, and it seemed an ideal situation, so I took it. He told me I could keep more of my money if I would help him write contracts and increase his exposure on the internet. I told him I wasn't experienced at either of these but was willing to learn.

I was not in the house long when I started to learn things about the owner. He was wired! I mean, he was very high-strung and would often pace around the house at an almost manic pace. He would stress over the smallest details. After a while, he began to bring me into his manic episodes, trying to get me to resolve his problems so he could calm down. I would sometimes try to help but often told him that I would not get involved and that he needed to resolve it on his own. After all, I had my own issues to deal with. I was on probation and needed to make sure I was consistently making it to work.

At work, I was doing well. I started as a floor production worker and now worked my way into running the second shift production floor. I was still running machines, but now I was also setting up scheduling for the employees, providing training as needed, and even interviewing and training new employees. It felt good to be back in a leadership role. The nice thing was that I had no access to money so that temptation would not exist although during that time I was not really tempted. It was the beginning of a quiet period for me, at least from a gambling perspective.

It was not so quiet on the home front. My landlord/roommate kept wanting me to get more and more involved in his business. And the more resistant I was, the more insistent he became. At the same time, he was developing an increasing dependence on painkillers, specifically OxyContin. He would go to different doctors then to the street to get his meds. He took them to "stay calm." He said it helped with his ongoing back pain but that it also helped to keep him focused when he felt out of control. To be honest, he was not far from the truth. He was much calmer when he was on his painkillers but was also developing an increased dependency. This dependency got continually worse until one day, at a convenience store, he had taken so much OxyContin that his heart stopped, and he dropped right there in the store. I found this out through someone he had worked with and went almost immediately to the hospital to check on him. I was told his heart had stopped for almost five minutes. When I went to see him, he was on a breathing tube and unconscious. He stayed that way for a few days and eventually woke up. After he was awake, I went to see him again. He thanked me for coming to see him then told me I needed to get him more OxyContin and sneak it into the hospital. I refused, and he proceeded to tell me I owed him that much for letting me live in his home. I left the hospital that day, packed everything I had into my car, and left.

I took all of my belongings and moved into a motel room not too far from work until I could find a new place to live. I was doing better financially, and not gambling, so I knew I could upgrade from where I was. The motel was inexpensive and not the highest quality, but it was livable and served my purpose while I searched. It took me almost two weeks to find a new place to live. It was a second-floor apartment about ten minutes from where my mother lived and about a half hour from work. I really liked it, so I agreed. He wanted a security deposit but agreed to give me a month to come up with it. Between the security deposit and the need for furniture for my new apartment, I decided to apply for a loan. I knew this could be dangerous territory for me. I also knew, given my past, it wasn't going to be easy. But I did find a lender who would give me a couple thousand dollars. It was at a pretty high interest, but I needed the cash and agreed to the terms. I gave my new landlord the security deposit and picked up some furniture for my new place.

The Calm Before the Storm

I moved into my new apartment in the spring of 2011. I was well established at my job, which I had for almost two years, and was doing well in my second shift leadership role. I enjoyed the balance I had. I got to work around 2:00 PM and left at 11:00 PM Monday through Friday. I could get up around eight in the morning and enjoy some of the day before I went into work. Plus, if I needed to get things done, I could. I was making my monthly probation appointments and was making my restitution payments on time. I was paying my loan on time as well. It didn't leave me with a ton of money, but it left me with enough to be able to go to the bar and restaurant across the street on the weekends and enjoy my downtime.

When I wasn't hanging out across the street, I would spend quite a bit of time on the deck I had thrown together in my backyard. This was just a pallet floor with a couple of tiki torches, a small grill, and a fence to keep the outside world out. It was peaceful for me. I also started to enjoy watching baseball again. I grew up outside of Philadelphia and have been a lifelong Phillies fan. So I started watching the games. I got along well with my neighbors in the apartment building. We would get together on my deck and grill dinner and just enjoy a few beers together. What I was not doing was gambling. I had no desire to gamble. I think a big part of that was due to the fact that I really wasn't accountable to anyone but me, and at the time, I was being very honest with me. So I felt no pressure, no stress, no anxiety. I would have periodic phone calls with my children. It felt good to be able to talk to them regularly. I would send them gifts on their birthday or holidays. My daughter was intrigued by my writing and would ask me for pointers because she had an interest at the time.

One of the things I decided to do during this time was build my network of friends. I was using Facebook more frequently and connecting with people I hadn't spoken with in a long time. One day I was reaching out to some people and decided to reach out to the girl I had dated in high school. She was the girl I dated in my senior year that I let go midway through that year then dated a few years later before she decided to let me go because she was interested in someone else. I had no motive in reaching out to her other than to continue to expand my group of friends. I was enjoying the increased social contact since I didn't have a huge network of friends nearby. She accepted my request, and we connected for the first time in a lot of years.

I was at work. I was sitting in my car during my lunch break, having a cigarette. I get a knock on the window. I look and see my old landlord and roommate, the one I had left in the hospital, standing there. I rolled down the window and he said hi. I said hi back and asked him what he was doing there. He said that he had been trying to find me to apologize for the way he treated me both while I lived there and while he was in the hospital. He said what he asked of me was unfair. I did not disagree. He asked if I might be willing to forgive him. I said yes, I would. We spoke for a while. During the conversation, he mentioned that the apartment that was attached to his house was open and available. I really liked that little apartment. It was basically an efficiency with some extra space. It had a glass block wall shower and a little room in the back. I asked him how much. He quoted me $200 a month, less than what I was spending, and that included cable, electric, and water. I told him I would get back to him soon, knowing too well I was going to say yes.

My landlord wasn't happy when I told him I'd be moving out, but I wasn't on a lease, so there was not a lot he could do about it. I had already taken off a few days leading up to the July 4 weekend in 2011. It would be the first multiday vacation I had since I was in the Army. It felt good. It felt normal, and I would now be spending part of it moving. During this time, I was also having more conversations with my old girlfriend from high school. We spoke on the phone one afternoon, and I got to meet her son. He was seventeen at the time.

While on that conversation, she asked if I'd like to come out to their place for July 4. They were having a picnic and later that evening was an orchestra concert at the local minor league baseball stadium. I said sure and that it sounded like fun. Finding her house was easy. She had inherited her parents' house when they passed away. It was the same house where I used to visit her when we were in high school. I drove out and met them for the picnic. It was strange to see her after all those years. I enjoyed the picnic and the concert. I also noticed I enjoyed her company. So later that evening, before I left, I told her I had fun and hope we could do it again. Well, we did.

The Love of My Life

Not even a week after I had gone to my high school sweetheart's place for a picnic, we were together again. This time she invited me over to watch a movie and hang out. Again, it was quite enjoyable. This time I could feel the attraction between us. It was kind of hard to deny. We talked and laughed and had a great time. I drove home that night with a smile on my face. I felt very connected to her, and I felt the connection she had with me. This was very different from the woman I was with a few years earlier. This felt real. The next morning, I called and officially asked her if we could date. She very quickly replied yes. That was the beginning of us.

I stayed in my apartment while we dated. I would mostly drive to her place on the weekend. I would sleep on the couch to set a good example for her son. But we basically did everything together. We would go to his high school band events. We met and visited her family and got to know them. I introduced her to my family, and she got to know them. Not too long into our relationship, I sat with her on her front porch and told her about my gambling addiction. I told her about my struggles in the military and about my struggles when I got out. I told her about the things I had done, including the theft and probation I was under. I told her a lot of truths about me. I also withheld a lot of truths and lied about a few things. I lied about my time in the military. I basically embellished my service to make myself look more "heroic." It's a shame really because other than the wrongdoings, I'm very proud of my service. But I did not have the confidence in myself to share that. I wanted her to stay with me and felt the best way to do it was to paint the best possible picture of myself that I could. I also lied about money. I was doing well with the loan I had taken out, but she was very particular about money.

I lied about having the loan. That would come back to haunt me down the road. It also set up a crash and burn that could have been easily avoided. What made matters worse was that she told me about relationships where she had been lied to and that the truth was one of her biggest expectations from a relationship. I nodded and agreed— the whole time I was holding secrets.

I put my lies on the back burner. We were doing well, and our relationship was blossoming. I remember thinking a few times that I needed to say something. But the thought of her reaction kept me from stepping up and doing what, in hindsight, I should have done right away. So I kept my mouth shut and kept enjoying the relationship. In 2012, I took out another loan. This one was to buy the ring I was going to propose with. Again, I didn't say anything. But by this time, I had talked her into giving me control of the finances. I did this by saying I wanted to prove myself by taking on more responsibilities regarding money. I believed this, or at least I had convinced myself I believed it. I got control of the money and could move things around as I saw fit.

In September of 2012, I proposed. It was a wonderful event that I had planned for weeks and took place at our favorite botanical garden. Her son held on to the ring until the right moment then I got down on one knee and proposed. Despite the lying I was doing and the things I withheld, I truly loved this woman and wanted to be married to her very badly. I started to convince myself I could pay off my loans before she knew what was happening. I was just blissful to be engaged to her, and she seemed to be overjoyed to be engaged to me. On the surface, we had the perfect relationship.

While we were engaged, I enrolled in online college courses through the VA. They paid for my courses and gave me a monthly stipend on top of that. I told my fiancée the stipend was for books and other course materials. This was partially true. I actually needed much less than what they were giving me, so I used the rest to pay down my loan. On top of all of this, my bank offered me a credit card with the highest limit I had ever had, $5,000. So I took it and again didn't say anything. I would take her out to dinner or shopping. When she would ask if we could afford it, I'd simply say, "Yep, no problem. We got it." I was putting all of this into a spreadsheet budget. I would put the numbers in that she would expect to see and move money around, so the account total matched the budget. I was beginning to do some of the manipulative things I did in my gambling addiction, but I would think, *I'm not gambling. I'm doing okay.* This, of course, was an excuse I would give myself to justify what I was doing. Slowly but surely, Mr. Hyde was awakening.

In October of 2014, we were married. With the exception of the birth of my children, it still stands as the happiest day in my life. She was, and still is, the love of my life. She was and is my soulmate. She loved me with all of her heart and trusted me without question. I loved her with all of my heart and was digging slowly into a hole that I knew would eventually come back to haunt me. But in that moment, it was bliss, so the rest could wait. I would figure a way out before I had to say anything. I just knew it.

2019

The marriage went on, and our love continued to grow. So did my debt. Four and a half years into our marriage, the money I was making from the VA didn't cover the loan and the credit card. I found myself taking out a second loan to keep the first lender satisfied. But how would I pay the second loan? And what about the credit card? I applied for and got approved for a second credit card. With that, I paid off the first one and bought myself some time. I applied for yet another small loan then another. I was digging in deeper. I was beginning to manipulate money like a juggler at the circus. I was also now beginning to take some other steps. I would find a reason to leave work early whenever I could. This was so I could check the mail before anyone got home. Because of where the mailbox was, at the end of a long lane, I was able to establish a habit that made me the main mail retriever. But with the amount of loans and credit cards I was getting into, I became more and more paranoid about anyone getting to the mail before I did. On the rare occasions that I didn't get the mail, I would have anxiety attacks until I found out that either no one had checked it or there was nothing to worry about.

In the summer of 2019, my debt was beginning to reach a peak. My wife was going on a trip to Texas to see her son. She would be there for a week. As soon as she left, I went to a loan company and leveraged my truck, which we had paid off the year before, so I could get a pretty big loan, about $17,000. I would use this loan to pay off a bunch of my smaller debts and get the runaway train I had created back on the tracks. But instead of doing that, I made a decision that took me down the rabbit hole even further. I took the money I had gotten and drove to a casino. It had been quite a few years since I'd been to a casino. But I thought I could turn that money into enough to pay quite a bit more off and maybe even get myself back to zero. Mr. Hyde was definitely back. I drove to that casino, lying to my wife and telling her I was going to see my father, and blew almost two-thirds of that $17,000. I gambled for many hours that day. It did not feel like it did years before. It felt dirty, but also necessary. The more money I pissed away that day, the more compelled I felt to stay and try to win it back until I finally reached a point where I had enough and packed it in. That day in 2019 is the last time I had ever set foot in a casino. I went home depressed, angry, embarrassed, and filled with shame. I had just taken a bad situation and made it quite a bit worse.

Last Desperate Reach and the Fall

The fall of 2019 was settling in. Leaves were turning and falling. The days were getting shorter and the temperatures colder, and I was becoming more and more desperate. I was becoming more irritable and got short in conversations with my wife. I would snap at her. She noticed and would point it out, and I would give some quick bullshit excuse. I was applying for more loans, but by now, I was in so deep and had fallen behind enough that no one would take me, except for a payday loan place. I reluctantly took the payday loan knowing their payback terms were much shorter than traditional loans and that their interest rates were ridiculous. I was also starting to fall behind on our household bills. This was something I was able to manage for years without falling behind. I had faithfully made these payments on time until that fall.

I was manipulating money, time, and the truth on an ongoing basis by this point. I became so desperate that I started to pay attention to philanthropists on social media. These were people that would share their wealth to help those less fortunate. Some of these people were legitimate. The fact is very few were or are legitimate. So I began to dive in and reach out in a last-ditch effort to magically fix my problem. Instead, I got connected to a scammer. I'm frankly very embarrassed to talk about what I did for this scammer because I knew better while I was doing it. But my gambling mind had fully returned by this point. I actually felt some excitement rushing to the mailbox or creating the next lie to see how long I could hold off the inevitable. This scammer had me buy gift cards then give him the numbers with the promise of a big return. The big return turned out to be a fake check that never made it into the bank. I was already drained of money and lost an additional three grand in my feverish endeavor.

It was December, and by now, I had started carrying a knife with me. This was a buck knife I had gotten from the American Legion. I kept it razor sharp and in my pocket at all times because if my wife had suddenly started to realize what was happening and started to question me. I was going to walk to the back of my property and use that knife to end everything. I once again had an exit plan. I was able to get one last department store credit card, which allowed me to get gifts for Christmas. I don't remember being very present at all during Christmas. I just remember drinking a lot and thinking about how I was going to end it. The same held true for New Year's Eve.

In the first week of January 2020, I went to a drugstore and bought the strongest weight loss pills I could get my hands on. I took several of them one night. My heart raced. My face turned bright red. I could not sleep. That was about it. Apparently, I had not taken enough of these to finish the job. I was once again at a point in my life where I had done so much damage, I didn't think it could ever be fixed. This time I did it to the woman I love with all of my heart. It was Friday, the third of January. I took the day off work and told my wife I was very sick. I set myself up on my loveseat, put on a blanket, turned on the TV (which I didn't really watch), and began the week-end-long process of deciding if I wanted to live or die.

After Gambling

Confession

On January 6, 2020, I got up, got showered, got dressed, kissed my wife, and told her I was off to work. I waited until she left then got into my truck and drove myself to my regional VA medical center. I walked into the emergency room, sat down at the check-in, and told them I was suicidal and needed to be checked in. They told me someone would be with me shortly, and I was not to go anywhere. I told them I needed to step outside and make a phone call first. They could see me outside, so they said okay. I went out. I made two calls. The first was to a longtime friend who was in recovery. He ran an online recovery support group, which I had never attended. I told him what I was doing and that I was scared to death. He assured me I was doing the right thing and asked me to reach out to him the next time I was able. The next call would be to my wife.

I stared at my phone for a few minutes. What I was about to do was to be one of the most painful moments of my life, and a moment I will remember until the day I die. My wife trusted everything I said. She may have questioned on occasion, but she always trusted. She thought I was her rock, and she was mine, and that we pretty much shared everything. Early on in our relationship, I had told her about my struggles with gambling. As far as she knew, those days were behind me. But I had pretty much lied to her throughout our entire relationship. I manipulated situations by doing things like taking over the finances and changing the conversation when talks of money came up. I took out loans and credit cards and snuck to the mailbox to make sure she never knew. I went through eight and a half years living this lie and her never knowing or believing she had a reason to question me. The only things she ever really asked of me in our relationship was to be honest. Now I had to tell her what I had done.

I knew if I was truly going to get myself into recovery that I had to tell her what I had done. She was at work. She answered the phone and could immediately hear the distress in my voice. I had tears streaming down my face, knowing what I was about to do and knowing it could very well mean the end of our relationship. I told her where I was. I also told her why I was there. I don't remember the exact conversation, but I remember saying I had gambled again and that I had taken out several loans and credit cards and that I had lied to her. As the conversation went on, I could feel the shock. I could feel the betrayal. I could feel the pain. It was nearly unbearable for me, so I can't begin to imagine how it was for her. We spoke for a bit more then I told her I needed to get myself into the hospital and that I would reach out as soon as I could. To my surprise, she said okay and told me she loved me. I didn't expect that. I was expecting a "don't bother" followed by a click. I would not have blamed her a bit had she done that.

I got admitted to an acute psychiatric ward at the VA. I told admissions I had a desire to hurt myself, which guaranteed my admission. I didn't know what else to do. I knew I really didn't want to hurt myself in that moment. I also knew I needed to do something drastic to stop and figure out how I was going to move forward. I was able to call my employer. My boss was very kind and told me to do what I needed to do. I got admitted and given a room. My clothing was taken from me, and I was given a set of scrubs that didn't fit and a pair of socks with grips on the bottom. It felt undignified, but again I didn't care. All of my possessions were taken from me. I was locked in and not going anywhere. Later that day, I was given phone access. I called my wife. The call was awkward at best. She asked how I was, and I just said I was okay for the moment. I asked how she was, and she said she didn't know. That's how day one ended.

In the spring of 2019, my daughter and her husband moved up from South Carolina and moved in with us. He was looking for work in Pennsylvania, and they would be looking for a house after a few months. In November of 2019, they told us that we were to be grandparents. It was a shock to me, but I was also very happy. Now, in January of 2020, I ran the risk of destroying the relationship it had taken so many years to rebuild with my daughter. A few days into my stay at the VA, my wife and my daughter both came for a visit. By this point, my wife was showing more anger toward me. She just couldn't understand how this could happen. She wanted answers. I had written what had happened with a rubber pencil on some note-book paper. I gave it to her when they came. She was not impressed. She wanted more, lots more. I just didn't know how to give it all then and was still holding up barriers. I was still shielding myself despite knowing that was the worst thing I could do. My daughter had writ-ten a note to me. She expressed some of what she was feeling when she was there but went much deeper in the note. She said that she loved me, and that she understood the struggles of going through mental health issues, but that what I did to them was not acceptable, and that I needed to commit fully to my recovery or I ran the risk of losing her and hopes of any relationship with my grandchild. While those were not the exact words, that was the message I received.

It hurt. The conversation with my wife hurt. I could feel her hurt, confusion, and anger, and it was agonizing. I had done this! I had created this. My wife came back a few days later and met with me and my psychiatrist. One of the things I remember is her anger over the fact that I didn't show more remorse. I felt remorse. I felt more remorseful than I probably ever had. But I struggled to show it. During that visit, we reached out to contact the director of the VA gambling treatment program in Ohio. I wanted to get back into this program. We spoke briefly and set up an appointment for a more detailed screening once I left the VA that I was in. She said it was likely I would be admitted and soon.

Back Home

When I got released from the VA, I drove myself home. I remember it being a cold snowy day. I got home and my wife was there. She had printed out a detailed credit history and wanted to go through it with me line by line so she could understand exactly what I had done and exactly how much damage needed to be repaired. It took a couple of hours, but we got through it. That exercise did not make the dynamic between us any better. She made it very clear that she wanted me to go to the VA gambling treatment program because she felt I needed it but also because she needed time to be without me so she could decide what she wanted. It was a very honest and very legitimate request on her part. I already knew I wanted and needed the VA program, so the decision was very easy. I did a screening with the director of the program. This was at the beginning of the second week in January. She told me I was in and that my cohort would begin at the start of February and run through the first week of March.

Before I went into the VA treatment program, a few things needed to take place. First, I turned all of my finances over to my wife. I was already more than willing to do this, but she made it a stipulation if we wanted our marriage to continue. I gave her all of my credit cards. I shut down my bank accounts and moved my pay over to an account she had set up. I turned over control of my cell phone account and pretty much anything that had anything to do, directly or indirectly, with money. I reached out to my friend Jeff, the first person I had called before calling my wife when I was at the VA. He ran (and still runs) an online problem gambling support group. I asked him if I could get involved and he did not hesitate. He gave me days and times for meetings, and I was on a meeting within two days. I also attended two Gamblers Anonymous meetings within my first week back. My wife and sister-in-law came with me for the first meeting because there was also supposed to be a Gam-Anon meeting that day.

Gam-Anon is for loved ones of people struggling with a gambling addiction. There was no Gam-Anon meeting being held that day, so the members of Gamblers Anonymous agreed and invited them to sit in on that meeting. At the end of the meeting, a gentleman who had been with GA for many years looked me in the eyes, in front of my wife, and said, "Tell her everything. Tell her before the sun comes up tomorrow." I will never forget that. And while I did leave some things out that did not come up until later, I told her more than I had ever told anyone. We went to another meeting later that week. That meeting had an active Gam-Anon meeting. We have both attended that meeting regularly since that first one we attended in early 2020. I also sat down with my boss from work and told him everything that he needed to know and that I would be going away for a month. He said he would have never known I was struggling and that it never impacted work, so I had nothing to worry about there. He helped me get my benefits started for my time away. This is the disease. I was destroying my life, and absolutely no one knew it.

Cleveland...Again

It was February 4 of 2020, and I was back in Cleveland. I was at a different hospital. The program had moved from an old VA facility in Brecksville, Ohio, to the main VA hospital in Cleveland. I parked, grabbed all of my luggage, and made my way to the offices where the director and her staff worked. The director came out and greeted me with a hug. She and I had never really lost contact since the last time I was there and had done some speaking engagements together. She turned me over to a peer who had recently completed the program. He took me to the VA domiciliary where I was given a room and told the rules of the road for living there. The next morning, we were introduced to our cohort and to the counselors with whom we would be working for the next five weeks.

I was settling into my treatment. I got to know the other eight veterans in my cohort and was getting to know my counselor. She was young and seemed relatively new to the field at first. But as I got to know her, I came to realize she was very good at what she did and genuinely cared about me and the other veterans on her caseload. The other counselors seemed the same way. They were all quite passionate about their work. It seemed the director had selected a team that had a similar vision to her own and that served those of us in the group quite well. The group was made up of men and women, from all different branches of service, and from different eras of service ranging from Vietnam to the most recent conflicts in Iraq and Afghanistan. We also all had different things that drew us into gambling. But we all had something in common. We were all looking to heal from our addiction. That common bond, along with a dedicated team and a great curriculum, made for a very good experience. Much like the first time I had gone to the gambling treatment program, I was asked early on what I wanted from the program. My response was very different. This time I simply said that I had a grandchild on the way and that I wanted that grandchild to simply know me as grandpa, not grandpa who gambled or lied or was never there, just grandpa. That's my wish. That's my legacy. I also talked about the devastation I had caused with my wife and about my desire to work to regain her trust because she is that person. She is my heart and soul, and I wanted to recover for us.

I struggled quite a bit in the first few weeks of treatment with the state of my marriage. I even talked about my fear several times in groups. I found out I was definitely not alone. I shared my fears of getting home from treatment and finding everything I owned on the front porch. That genuinely scared me at first. Then something began to shift. I knew I wanted to save and keep my marriage. I knew how much I loved my wife. I also began to come to an acceptance that no matter what happened when I got home, I had to stay strong in my recovery. The longer I was in the treatment program, the stronger I began to feel. I was starting to uncover some of the lifelong struggles that lay beneath my addiction. I started to allow myself to become uncomfortable with feelings I didn't want to have and to just let them be until they passed. I began to discover who I was and what was creating barriers for me. The more that happened, the less obsessed I became with saving my marriage. I began to reach a level of acceptance that my wife may decide that this was a path she didn't want to walk with me. Don't get me wrong. I would still fight for the marriage. But I also felt much stronger in the knowledge that if she ultimately decided to leave me, despite the hurt I would continue to work on me. That is honestly something I had not previously experienced, and it marked a pretty huge change in my recovery. My wife and I talked on a regular basis while I was there. She was still struggling with where she was with us, but it felt more and more like she was becoming willing to give us a chance. But I had to do my part. I had to continue on the path I had started on January 6 of that year.

About midway through my treatment, an amazing thing happened. I had been reading a book about finding the deeper and better version of ourselves (Dyer 1991). One of the exercises in the book talks about things that may have haunted us in our past and about making peace with these things. The exercise was to find a tough time from the past. It could be a traumatic incident or a painful breakup or fight. Just find something that was very painful at the time and still brings up panful memories when we think about it today. Now, take the "me" that exists today and gently stand next to and put my arms around the "me" that existed when this incident took place. Gently comfort that "me" and let them know things will be and are okay. When I read this, it seemed like a pretty interesting exercise. I didn't know I would actually use it.

One morning, I was in my room, getting ready for the day. My roommate was not there. It was just me. I had my phone on a music streaming station and was playing music from my "favorites" playlist. My wedding song came on. In that moment, I lost it. All of the regret and shame and guilt from everything that I had done to my wife came rushing forward in an emotional tidal wave, and I began crying uncontrollably. I knew I needed to do this, but it felt nearly unbearable. Then, the "me" that was beginning to feel healthier, the "me" that was beginning to forgive myself showed up and gently put an arm around the "me" that was in an emotional breakdown and simply said, "I'm here. Let it happen." It's hard to describe how that felt. I was releasing a ton of feelings yet felt comforted doing it. This lasted for about a half hour. I calmed down, regained myself, and felt like a weight had been lifted. It was a pretty amazing thing to experience.

March 2020: Back Home

In early March of 2020, I completed my treatment in Cleveland. I was feeling stronger than I had in a long time. There was a huge difference between leaving treatment in 2020 and when I left treatment in 2007. Back then, I knew I had a problem. This time I knew I was powerless unless I continued to stay ahead of my feelings and continued to work on me. As I left treatment, a new challenge was beginning to present itself. I was, as we all were, hearing more and more about the emergence of a virus that had originated in China. This virus, COVID-19, was shutting down businesses and impacting hospitals all over. It even affected the VA treatment program I had just left. Not long after I left, the residential program was shut down, and it went completely online. I have to say I'm grateful to have been able to be there for treatment.

When I got back home, the relationship with my wife was still strained, but it appeared to be slowly on the mend. We talked more. I began to open up more and to get more honest about how I was feeling. We began to attend our Wednesday Gamblers Anonymous and Gam-Anon meetings again. It was a night for us to have some time to just talk. The ride to the meeting is almost a half hour, so it gave us time to check in and see where things were. It still does. I was still attending my online gambling support group meetings. I was home more because my employer starting to have all nonproduction employees work from home because of the onset of the pandemic. I was a safety manager, so I could not be at home all of the time. But when I was not actively engaged in a facility, I was working from home. This gave me the opportunity to attend more meetings.

One of the things my wife and I agreed to was that none of my gambling debt would be paid from our house money. I was going to have to get another job to pay down this debt. This would allow us to continue moving forward financially and would also help solidify the desire to not go back to my addiction because of the hours needed to pay down this debt in a timely manner. While I was in Cleveland, I had reached out to the addiction treatment center I had interned with during the time I was in school for my master's degree.

In April of 2020, I got an interview with the center, and they offered me a part-time job as a supervised therapist. I would be working at a residential treatment facility, working with patients struggling with drug and alcohol addictions. Because of the hourly rate I was offered to start, I would only need to work two nights and a full Saturday each week. Unfortunately, I couldn't start right away. The center was on a work freeze because of COVID, and I would not be able to start until late May. I had already set up a plan with an agency that would work to pay down all but one of my debts. I had a payment plan with them that would start as soon as I started working. I also made arrangements with the loan company where I had leveraged my truck. They settled for a small payment each month. I debated letting my loan go into default and letting my truck get repossessed. At that point, my credit rating was in the toilet anyway. But after conversations with my wife and VA counselor, I decided it was best to take responsibility and pay it off.

I kept the counselor I had in Cleveland. We would meet weekly, over the phone, then biweekly, and eventually monthly. In the meantime, I found a counselor at my local VA. My wife and I also attended marriage counseling. I think it was good for us. My wife felt like it wasn't enough, but she was feeling more connected at Gam-Anon and felt that was helping. I had regular conversations with my debt collectors until my job started, and I was able to build up enough money to start making payments. I guess my timing was fortunate because most of the debt collectors were lenient given that we were in the middle of a pandemic. I was able to start making regular payments that July.

While attending my online gambling support group, I was introduced to Brian. Brian hosted a podcast to talk about gambling addiction. He had guests who had gone through addiction, as well as advocates, clinicians, and others. One of the podcasts he did was a weekend therapy with gamblers from all over. I was invited to be a part of it and happy to do so. We would pick a topic and talk about our own journey related to that topic. After one of those meetings, I asked if he could stay online for a moment after the meeting. I asked him about an idea I had to do a podcast similar to his but focusing on military service members and veterans. One of the things I remembered from my days gambling in the Army was that no one really knew about the addiction, or what to do with me, and that might be a great way to raise awareness and let service members and veterans know they were not alone, which is how I felt until I found my recovery. He thought that was a great idea, and from that, *Fall In: The Problem Gambling Podcast for Military Service Members and Veterans* was born. I feel like it has done a great deal to help raise awareness but still has a long way to go.

One More Mistake

It was June of 2020. We were packing the truck to make our annual trek to the amusement park and campground we camped at every Father's Day weekend. My wife got a call. It was from the debt negotiation company to whom I had handed my debt. There was some debt information they brought up that I had neglected to bring up with my wife when I set everything up. It was a payday loan that did not show up in the credit report. When she told me about it, I said it wasn't a big deal. It was a small loan, and I made sure it was included. The reality was I had essentially lied by not telling her. She would always ask, "Is that everything?" and when I would say, "Yes," she'd say "Are you sure?" So, in plain words, I lied. She was mad. Okay, she was furious. It seemed like we were making good progress, and this was a huge setback.

We went to the campground and set up. We went out to dinner. As we were sitting down, she asked me a question. I honestly don't remember the question. I just remember her response when I answered her. It was "That's a nice story." I got up and started to storm out of the restaurant because I was mad that she would treat me that way. But about five steps into my storm, I stopped dead in my tracks. I thought about what reason she would have to believe me after everything I had done. I turned around, and I sat back down. We began a conversation that went on all through dinner and felt like it restarted the healing process. The next morning, I called my sponsor. He called me an idiot (in the nicest way) and stressed the importance of being totally honest, even when it felt very uncomfortable. I knew he was right, of course. I had told her just about everything but left out one little detail. The problem is that what seemed like one little detail to me was just one more lie to her. How could she trust anything I said if that's what I was still willing to do? I pulled her aside and told her that. She agreed, and the rest of the weekend went much more smoothly. As I was going through all of this, I remembered the words of the gentleman at the first GA meeting I attended back in January, when he said tell her everything, and tell her before the sun comes up. Those words rang in my ears. They still do. It's an anchor point for me when I feel like holding back.

Over the course of the next year or so, I became consistent with GA meetings. I started working at the treatment center and was able to get them to add in a gambling awareness group where I could talk to patients being treated for drug or alcohol addiction about gambling as an addiction. I feel blessed to have found that job. It has been an additional source of recovery for me. Oh yeah, and my debt has gotten paid down as well. I started advocating again, speaking for radio programs, for groups raising awareness, and even for a TV news segment. The sharing for me is a way to stay anchored. Recovery this time around looks very different for me. I feel healthier, mentally and emotionally, than I ever have. I stay firmly connected to my recovery, and I live today. I don't worry about the future because it will take care of itself.

As I write this, I now have two granddaughters. They simply know me as grandpa or as I'm called "Grampy." My relationship with my wife is far stronger than it was when the house of cards fell. I will say it's probably not where either of us would like it to be yet. I did a lot of damage, and she will likely never put the trust in me she once did. She still questions a lot of what I do and say, and rightly so, but I just answer honestly and let her decide what she wants to believe or not. The more I do that, the more it feels like she believes me again. We love each other very much. I am truly grateful that she has decided to stay with me on this journey. It makes a huge difference to me. I still work part-time at my treatment center. I often tell patients my day job pays my bills, and my part-time job fuels my passion. I have not decided if I will continue to work there after my final payment is made. The debt negotiator, which covered most of my debts, is paid off and I have but a few truck payments to make yet.

Time will tell. I feel like a different person. I feel more comfortable in my own skin. I still have bouts of depression now and then. I still have times I don't want to talk about things. I'm still a perfectionist, and I still struggle with my ego now and then. I'm not sure these things will ever fully go away. What has changed is the way I work through these things. I allow myself to get uncomfortable. I very purposefully share what's going on with me, even if it might seem trivial or mundane. I do this because if I practice the small things, I'm more willing to share the bigger ones.

I have roadblocks in place. I still have no control over my money. It's actually quite blissful for me because my wife doesn't mind taking care of our money, and I don't worry about temptation. I get what I want as long as it's not overly impulsive. The truth is, other than those closest to me, and now you because you just read this, no one would really know I don't carry or control money. I attend meetings every week. I don't attend the online meetings right now because my schedule is quite busy, and I work very hard to keep a balance. But I don't lose sight of the fact that I need my meetings to stay connected. I found a connection to be a huge key to my ongoing recovery. I can't do it alone. I don't want to do it on my own. I enjoy the sharing.

The Tools of My Recovery

I feel that since the events that happened on January 6 of 2020 that I am really in recovery for the first time. I had quiet periods after my first visit to treatment in 2007. I also learned quite a bit about the addiction and the things I can do to help stay free from the addiction. I even had a fairly good period of time free from gambling. But I never really stepped into my recovery. So you may ask, "Okay, so what makes this time different?" It's actually a very good question. The very first thing I would say is that I came to a couple of realizations. The first is that I didn't just have a gambling problem, I live with an addiction and am powerless over that addiction unless I do something every single day to stay in front of it. Second, I needed to come to grips with the fact that I need to be in recovery for me, first and foremost. Yes, I want to be in recovery for my wife, my children, my grandchildren, and all of the people who have meaning in my life. But if I don't do it for me, it's not real. As the old phrase goes, "you can't pour from an empty cup." Finally, I needed to begin to love, accept, and know the guy in the mirror. I am human. I am flawed. I am learning to accept that. As for the specific tools I use and always recommend for recovery, it comes down to three things: roadblocks, accountability, and connection.

Roadblocks are those things that kept and continue to keep me from being tempted to gamble. Many of these I've already mentioned, such as turning over my finances and access to money to my wife. Not everyone has someone who's as willing as she is to do this. My response to that is find someone to look over your shoulder. Find a payee to take charge of your money. Find someone. Another big roadblock for me was self-exclusion. I put myself on a list that bans me from casinos in my state. If I walk into these casinos, I'm technically trespassing. And while the self-exclusion system is not perfect, it's enough of a deterrent for me, combined with other roadblocks, to keep me from even thinking about going.

Accountability goes far beyond someone knowing where I am or what I'm doing at any given time. To me, that's more a roadblock than accountability. What I'm talking about is being accountable to who I am, to what I'm feeling, and to whatever comes up for me. While they don't happen very often anymore, I still get urges to gamble. I still feel the occasional swell of adrenaline when I see an ad or pass a casino. Being accountable means that I recognize those feelings when they come up and then share them so they can pass. Basically, I tell on myself. Keeping these feelings to myself can ultimately be dangerous, so I don't. Accountability also means being completely honest. It means saying something even when I feel uncomfortable saying it. I began to overcome this by adding a phrase. I would say to my wife, "I feel uncomfortable saying this, but I need to say it." She knows what that means. It means I'm allowing myself to reveal parts of myself I was never willing to reveal in the past. This is critical to my recovery because it allows me to let things go instead of bottling them up. It's also much easier to tell the truth than to lie because I don't have to remember what I said and if what I'm about to say contradicts it.

Finally, one of the most important discoveries I made in my recovery was the value of connection. We all have emotional crap that piles up sometimes, whether that leads to addiction or not. Sitting in a room or even on a Zoom call with people who are struggling with similar struggles, facing similar challenges, and have similar goals allows me to share the crap that piles up, which takes some of the power out of it. I often say now that the power of a roomful of people with a similar vision is far greater than any individual in that room. Connection is my higher power. It's a huge part of my strength. I will not ever be without some form of connection. Find the connection, whatever that connection is. To really begin to step into recovery, I asked myself a question. I was willing to go to great lengths to feed my addiction. How far am I willing to go to feed my recovery? That question helps guide me every day.

Roadblocks, accountability, and connection are the three main things I always emphasize when I'm asked about or am talking about recovery. But there's so much more to it for me. I discovered what doesn't work for me. Thinking "I've got this" simply doesn't work. As soon as I start thinking that way, I start acting that way. I let go of the connection and tools that keep me in recovery because I feel like I don't need them anymore. I do need them! These tools and these connections are absolutely essential to my recovery and will be for the rest of my life. That felt like a tall order when I first came to that realization. I was a bit stressed about having to work hard at recovery day after day. Here's the thing. That work has become less stressful as I get further into my recovery. The things I focused on almost hourly early in my recovery don't need to be hourly anymore. Yes, I have to stay focused on them. But the more I practice the tools of recovery, the more natural they become for me, and they become part of who I am. Have you ever tried a new workout regimen after not working out for several years? At first, it came to seem nearly impossible. But as you practice and build strength, endurance, and muscle memory, the process gets more manageable, even easier. The same holds true for recovery. Create "muscle memory" for recovery, and recovery becomes part of you.

Telling My Story

I started telling my story, in front of strangers, somewhere around 2015. I was asked to speak in front of senate staffers in Washington DC to help try to pass legislation to get better care for service members and veterans. I was scared and intimidated, but I knew I wanted and needed to do it. I had a small stack of index cards to help guide me through it. I spoke for about fifteen minutes. Afterward, several people came up to me to tell me how brave what I did was. Yes, I was nervous. But telling my story didn't feel like bravery to me. It felt liberating and it felt natural. I felt like I was sharing something that was not unique and prayed it would reach people who would do something with it. Since that time, I've told my story many times at conferences, informational briefs, webinars, TV news, podcasts, and more. The more I tell my story, the more connected I stay to my recovery. I've had several service members and veterans who were struggling reach out to me because of my story. Some of them are in recovery to this day. Some still struggle. But all of them discovered they are not alone. I will say telling your story is not for everyone. We need to be solid in our recovery before even looking into this. It was not the first time I did it, and I wonder if that contributed to my relapse. Also, it's important to remember that if you tell your story publicly, that doesn't go away, especially if it's online or for the media. But if you are strong in your recovery, and okay with living your recovery out loud, you could be a beacon of hope for someone else, and we pay it forward.

If you have the opportunity to learn about mindfulness, I highly recommend looking into it. Mindfulness has been thrown around recklessly by businesses and other places over recent years. The discovery of what it really is has been amazing for me. Basically, mindfulness is getting very aware of thoughts, feelings, body sensations, and whatever else comes up in this moment, right now. The key is to simply let these feelings, thoughts, sensations be. There's no judgment. There's no trying to make these things go away or do something with them. Just let them be. My journey into this process has taught me that by just letting feelings or thoughts be there, and be what they will be, they eventually pass. They pass without doing damage or making things worse or opening Pandora's box. They just pass, and when they pass organically, there's a feeling of liberation that goes with it. At least that feeling comes up for me. I've spoken to many others who feel the same way. There are many apps out there that can teach mindfulness. Taking the time to learn it could make a difference.

To bring it all home, let me say this. Each of us has a story to tell. Each of us has struggles that maybe we feel no one could understand. I felt that way early in my addiction. What I have discovered is that no matter what the struggle, someone out there gets it. Someone will understand and it takes reaching out to find that someone. To service members, veterans, or anyone out there struggling with a gambling addiction, you are not alone. Someone gets it. My story is one among many. As more of us begin to come forward and tell our stories, we will begin to reduce and hopefully remove the stigma that surrounds this disease. We will raise awareness. We will foster hope.

This is a story of hope.

Resources

The following is a list of resources for anyone who is seeking or knows someone who is seeking help for a gambling addiction. Some of these will be military and/or veteran-specific and some will be more broad-based.

- Operation Responsible Gambling—OPRG is a website created by the National Council on Problem Gambling. This site gives information on problem gambling as it relates to service members and veterans and also offers links to resources. It's found at https://operationresponsiblegambling.org.
- The National Council on Problem Gambling—Offers phone, email, and chat helplines as well as links to resources in many states: https://www.ncpgambling.org. 1-800-GAMBLER is the number for help.
- Podcasts—There are numerous podcasts about gambling and gambling addiction. Many of these are hosted by people who have lived through gambling addiction. These podcasts offer hope and often have links to resources. Among these are the following:
  - *Fall-In: The Problem Gambling Podcast for Military Service Members and Veterans*
  - *All In: The Addicted Gamblers Podcast*
  - *The Broke Girl Society*—with a focus on women and problem gambling
  - *The After Gambling Podcast*
  - *The Invisible Addiction*
  - *Hello, My Name is Craig*—Hosted by national sports commentator Craig Carton

- *Beyond the Bet*
- *The Hidden Addiction Podcast*
- *Ambitious Addicts, the Podcast*
- And more. Just search these names. Many of these podcasts are on most podcast platforms.

- Gamblers Anonymous—Gamblers Anonymous (GA) is a twelve-step, peer-run recovery program started in 1957. Go to https://www.gamblersanonymous.org for more information and to find nearby meetings.

- Smart Recovery—Is another peer-run recovery program. This program is not addiction-specific and is run on evidence-based principles. It can be found at https://www.smartrecovery.org.

- Department of Veterans Affairs Gambling Treatment Program—The Department of Veterans Affairs has the oldest residential gambling treatment program in the United States, located in Cleveland, Ohio. This program, which has been primarily residential, also offers virtual options. A second center was opened in Las Vegas, Nevada, in 2020. Ask a VA provider for more information or go to https://www.va.gov and search gambling addiction.

- State Problem Gambling Councils—Many states have councils that offer resources, including funded treatment resources for those struggling with a gambling addiction. Some states have veterans outreach personnel to help veterans navigate resources. Just search problem gambling council and your state to see what your state offers.

References

Dyer, Wayne W. 1991. *Your Sacred Self.* Harper-Collins.

About the Author

 Dave is an eleven-year veteran of the United States Army and is in recovery from a gambling addiction. Dave is the host of *Fall In: The Problem Gambling Podcast for Military Service Members and Veterans* and actively advocates for better education, screening, and treatment for gambling addiction among these groups. Dave has served on the military committee for the National Council on Problem Gambling.